Great Stories from Mormon History

Great Stories from Mormon History

Dean Hughes
and
Tom Hughes

Deseret Book Company
Salt Lake City, Utah

Library of Congress Cataloging-in-Publication Data

Hughes, Dean, 1943–
    Great stories from Mormon history / Dean Hughes and Tom Hughes.
       p.   cm.
    ISBN 0–87579–849–7
    1. Church of Jesus Christ of Latter-day Saints—History—Juvenile literature. 2. Mormon Church—History—Juvenile literature. [1. Church of Jesus Christ of Latter-day Saints—History. 2. Mormon Church—History.] I. Hughes, Tom, 1968–   . II. Title.
BX8611.H76   1994
289.3—dc20   94–8988
                                                                              CIP
                                                                              AC

Printed in the United States of America
10   9   8   7   6   5   4   3   2   1

Contents

1

Young Joseph's Leg Operation

In 1813, doctors had very few medicines to work with. They didn't even have aspirin. A simple fever or infection sometimes killed a person—especially a child. When people needed surgery, doctors had no way to put them to sleep first. Patients would drink a big glass of whiskey to deaden the pain, maybe bite down on a rag or stick, and the doctor would start cutting.

A good doctor was a fast doctor.

It was in those days, when Joseph Smith was seven years old, that he needed a good doctor. An epidemic of typhoid fever had struck Lebanon, New Hampshire, where Joseph lived. Typhoid can be controlled by modern medicines, but in Joseph's time it often killed its victims. Their insides would become infected and their tongues would turn black. Ulcers would form inside their bodies and then break out into huge sores on their skin.

All the Smith children—Alvin, Hyrum, Sophronia, Joseph, Samuel, William, and Catherine—one after another, caught the disease. Ten-year-old Sophronia almost died. After three months of treatment, her doctor gave up on her, and finally, she seemed to take her last breath. But Joseph, Sr.,

and Lucy, her parents, fell on their knees and pleaded with the Lord to spare her, and then Lucy grabbed Sophronia up in her arms and pressed her to her chest. Sophronia began to breathe again, and she recovered steadily from that day.

Joseph survived what seemed to be a mild case of the disease. He was sick for only two weeks. But after his recovery, he developed a bad pain in his shoulder. Joseph's doctor thought it was a sprain, even though Joseph didn't remember hurting himself. The doctor rubbed liniment—a sort of lotion often used in those days—on Joseph's shoulder. Then he applied another nice remedy: he pressed a hot shovel against the painful area. He assured Joseph that all would be well.

But he was wrong.

When the doctor returned some time later, he found that a large fever sore had developed near Joseph's shoulder blade. This time he used a knife. He cut the sore open. Lucy Smith said that more than a quart of pus oozed out.

The Smiths thought Joseph might be all right after that. But Joseph's trials were only beginning. No sooner had the pain left his shoulder than it seemed to shoot down his side and into his lower leg. That was how it felt to Joseph, anyway. What had really happened was that the disease had infected the bone in his leg.

Joseph's leg, below the knee, became huge from swelling, and the pain was almost more than he could stand. He was in agony for two weeks, with nothing at all to ease the constant ache. His mother, Lucy, nursed him and carried him around, even though Joseph was a good-sized boy for his age. And then Lucy got sick.

Joseph's thirteen-year-old brother, Hyrum, who would turn out to be loyal to Joseph throughout his life, took over.

He sat with Joseph almost all the time, day and night. Holding the sore part of Joseph's leg, he would press it to help relieve the pain. For a week Hyrum hardly slept, and Joseph held out the best he could.

Finally the doctor came again with his knife. He sliced Joseph's shin open, making a cut eight inches long while Joseph was wide awake to feel it all. The raw pain was terrible, but opening the leg this way did relieve the pressure. For a short time Joseph was able to rest. As soon as the cut began to heal, however, the pain returned.

The next time the doctor cut deeper and longer, from the knee most of the way to the ankle—and all the way down to the bone. Joseph could do nothing but scream and take the torture.

And the results were the same. The pain and swelling returned as soon as the cut began to heal.

Finally a group of surgeons and students from Dartmouth Medical School came to the Smith home. After examining the wound, they all agreed: to save Joseph's life, they would have to cut his leg off.

Joseph wouldn't hear of it. He told his parents he wouldn't let the doctors take his leg. He was young, but his mind was made up, and so his mother asked the doctors whether they couldn't just cut the diseased part of his leg bone away. The doctors talked things over and decided they would try. But it was not going to be a simple operation, and certainly not a quick one.

The doctors wanted Joseph to drink some liquor, and then they wanted to tie him to the bed with ropes to keep him still. But Joseph preferred to have his father sit on the bed and hold him. The doctors agreed to that, and so did Joseph's father. Joseph asked his mother to leave the room, and then he said he was ready.

The surgery was almost too horrible to imagine. The doctor cut the leg open again, and then he drilled into the bone, first on one side and then the other. Then he used forceps—an instrument like a pair of pliers—and broke away chunks of bone.

When the doctor chipped the first piece of bone, Joseph screamed out loud, which brought his mother running into the room. Joseph begged her to leave. But when the third piece broke loose, and Joseph screamed a third time, Lucy couldn't stand it. She burst into the room once again. This time the sight was so awful that she had to get out, and she didn't return until everything was over and the blood was cleaned up.

Still, the operation was a success. Joseph walked on crutches for almost three years, and he walked with a slight limp the rest of his life. But he kept his leg. More important, he showed the resolve—the strength and faith—that he was going to need to face a life of never-ending trials.

For further reading, see Lucy Mack Smith, History of Joseph Smith, by His Mother *(Salt Lake City: Bookcraft, 1958), pp. 54–58; Donna Hill,* Joseph Smith, the First Mormon *(New York: Doubleday, 1977), pp. 35–36.*

2

A Promise to a Hero

When Joseph Smith was growing up, he had a hero. His big brother Alvin, almost seven years older than Joseph, was a powerful young man and a hard worker. But he was also gentle and quiet. There was no one Joseph looked up to more than Alvin. Once, the two of them went to a boxing match together. These fights were bare-fisted scraps with very few rules. But this time, when one of the boxers got the better of the other, he began to gouge at his opponent's eyes. Alvin couldn't stand by and watch that. He charged in, grabbed the fighter by the collar and britches, and threw him out of the ring.

Joseph was proud to watch. His brother was not only big and strong, but he was good. He stood up for what was right.

When the Smith family moved to Manchester, New York, near Palmyra, Alvin worked with his father to clear trees from the land so they could farm it. Then he began to build a fine house for his parents and their family.

In the spring of 1820, at age fourteen, Joseph had a miraculous experience that would change his life. He entered a grove of trees near his family's farm and prayed to know what religion he should follow. Heavenly Father and Jesus Christ appeared to him and told him not to join any church, but to wait for a time when the true gospel would be revealed to him.

Joseph reported the entire experience to his family. His account was so simple and honest that they knew he was telling the truth. Alvin was especially moved by the story, and he was convinced that Joseph would come to be a great and important servant of the Lord.

A few years later, in 1823, the angel Moroni appeared to Joseph and told him about some plates of gold hidden in a hill. On the plates were the religious writings of an ancient people who had lived on the American continent. The angel promised Joseph that if he lived worthily, he would someday be allowed to translate the records. Alvin was fascinated to hear everything about this experience. He could hardly wait for the day when Joseph would begin his great work. Time and again, he reminded Joseph to be worthy of the blessing.

Joseph sometimes wondered whether Alvin shouldn't have been the one chosen to serve the Lord. Joseph, at age seventeen, suspected himself of being too playful and not serious enough for such an important work. He didn't even like to study the scriptures the way twenty-four-year-old Alvin did.

But then, not long after the angel Moroni visited Joseph the first time, Alvin fell ill. A doctor had given him a medicine called calomel, but Alvin could feel that it had gotten stuck in his intestines and was going to kill him. Other doctors tried other medicines, but nothing would dislodge the calomel, and Alvin grew worse. After four days, he called his family to him one at a time. He told his brothers and sisters to be loyal to each other and to look after their parents as they grew old.

When Joseph's turn came, he approached Alvin's bed quietly. Joseph's heart was breaking at the thought of losing his big brother. He couldn't hold the tears back. But he listened closely to what Alvin told him. "I want you to be a good boy," Alvin said, "and do everything in your power to obtain the Record." Alvin told Joseph to be faithful in keeping every commandment that was given him.

Joseph promised that he would. But at that moment he couldn't stand to think of life without Alvin.

The last child to come to Alvin's bedside was little Lucy, just two years old. When Alvin told her that he must "go away," she cried and clung to him so tightly that her mother could hardly pull her away.

Soon after Alvin said good-bye to his family, he died. Joseph agonized over the loss. But he never forgot Alvin's advice. And he held Alvin up as an example. His hero had died, but Alvin's goodness, his work habits, his nobility, his devotion to his family—these were qualities Joseph tried to develop in himself.

Joseph had promised an angel, and he had promised the Lord, that he would live the commandments. But he had also promised his big brother who had died, and he didn't want to let him down. During those difficult years as he waited to receive the plates, he never forgot his vow to his dying brother.

For further reading, see Lucy Mack Smith, History of Joseph Smith, by His Mother *(Salt Lake City: Bookcraft, 1958), pp. 86–89; Donna Hill,* Joseph Smith, the First Mormon *(New York: Doubleday, 1977), pp. 59–60.*

3

Parley P. Pratt's Conversion

Parley Parker Pratt was a young farmer who spent his evenings reading the Bible. He had gradually become convinced that the churches he had learned about were not teaching the pure gospel. He also felt sure that they didn't have the authority to act in the Lord's name. Praying and studying to try to find the truth, he felt the Spirit teach him and give him insights.

In the summer of 1830, The Church of Jesus Christ of Latter-day Saints was only a few months old. Parley Pratt had never heard of it. But he did know, from his studies and by the Spirit, that Christ would someday return to the earth, and he felt the need to warn people to repent and prepare the way. He decided he should go out and preach the principles he understood.

Parley and his wife, Thankful, had a home and a beautiful farm in Ohio. They would have to leave all that behind if Parley was to go where the Spirit led him. Thankful supported her husband and agreed that if the Spirit of the Lord told Parley to preach, he should preach.

Parley and Thankful sold their farm at a great loss. By the time they paid off their bills, they were left with only ten dollars. They decided to visit their families in and around Canaan, New York. Parley would start by teaching family and friends. After that, they would let the Spirit tell them where to go next.

It was a righteous plan, but the Lord had other things in mind for Parley. The Pratts were traveling to Canaan on a river boat. When it stopped in Rochester, New York, to take on passengers and supplies, Parley told to Thankful that the Spirit had prompted him to get off the boat at the next stop. He told her to continue on to her family home. "I will come soon," he told her, "but how soon I know not; for I have a work to do in this region of country."

Thankful knew her husband. There was no use arguing. When he heard the Spirit, he always listened. And so she went on without him.

Parley got off the boat in the little town of Newark, New York. It was still early in the morning when he stopped at a farmhouse, where a man named Mr. Wells invited him to breakfast. When Parley offered to preach that evening, Mr. Wells took him to meet some of the neighbors who might be interested. One of the people they met was a Baptist deacon named Mr. Hamlin.

Soon it was clear why the Lord had directed Parley to this place. Hearing that Parley was interested in religion, Mr. Hamlin told him about Joseph Smith and the Book of Mormon. As Parley listened to the story with great interest, he knew he had to read that book.

Mr. Hamlin told Parley to come back the next morning and he would show him a copy of the Book of Mormon. So Parley preached that night and then returned to Mr. Hamlin's home the next morning. He later wrote this about reading the Book of Mormon for the first time:

"I read all day; eating was a burden, I had no desire for food; sleep was a burden when the night came; I preferred reading to sleep. As I read, the spirit of the Lord was upon me, and I knew and comprehended that the book was true."

Parley decided he wanted to meet the young man who had discovered and translated this wonderful book. So he set out walking to Palmyra. As it had turned out, the Lord had led him to get off the boat just a few miles from the Smith farm.

When Parley reached the farm, he met a man who was driving some cows to a nearby pasture. He asked the man whether he knew Joseph Smith. The man said he did, but that Joseph had moved to Pennsylvania, about a hundred miles away. Parley wondered whether he could meet any of Joseph's family and learn more about the Book of Mormon and the newly formed church. At that point the man said that he was Hyrum Smith, the Prophet's brother, and he would be happy to tell Parley anything he wanted to know.

The two men talked until late that night. One of the things Parley told Hyrum was that he was searching for the authority to act in God's name. Hyrum told Parley about the priesthood that Joseph Smith and Oliver Cowdery had received from John the Baptist and from the apostles Peter, James, and John.

Parley was thrilled. He felt the truth of all he heard. He was amazed and thankful that in setting out to serve the Lord, he had been led almost immediately to the right place.

A few days later, Hyrum introduced Parley to Oliver Cowdery, who along with Joseph Smith had received the priesthood from the angels. Oliver baptized and confirmed Parley and then immediately ordained him an elder. Parley now possessed the authority he had been seeking.

A few weeks later, Parley joined his wife, Thankful, as they had agreed. He was able to preach to and baptize several friends and family members, including his younger brother Orson.

Parley P. Pratt continued on the path where the Spirit led him. He served many missions, was ordained an apostle when the Quorum of the Twelve was first organized, and served the Lord for the rest of his life. And all this began because he had the courage to step off a boat for no other good reason than that he knew it was what God wanted him to do.

For further reading, see Parley P. Pratt, Autobiography of Parley P. Pratt *(Salt Lake City: Deseret Book, 1975), pp. 33–42.*

4

A Home in Ohio

In the winter of 1830–1831, all the elk disappeared from the plains of North America. It was a cruel season, with snow lying four feet deep. Elk and other large animals became trapped when they broke through the crust on the snow. Wolves, light and quick, could run across the crust and attack the helpless animals.

That winter, early in January, Joseph and Emma Smith, along with Edward Partridge and Sidney Rigdon, set out from New York for Kirtland, Ohio. Joseph had received a revelation that Church members should gather to Kirtland, but the revelation didn't promise that the trip would be easy. And it wasn't, especially for Emma. They were making the three-hundred-mile journey in a horse-drawn sleigh. The sleigh was crowded, the cold was harsh, and Emma was expecting a baby.

Emma Hale Smith was twenty-six years old at that time. She had already learned that her marriage to Joseph, the young prophet, was going to require great sacrifices. Her parents had never been happy with her choice of a husband. To them, it seemed that Joseph was too concerned with his translation of the Book of Mormon to provide well for a family.

Their worries might have been justified. Although Joseph was a hard-working man who could have made a good living, he had a calling to help carry out the restoration of the gospel. That work pulled him away from his daily labor. Members of the new church were willing to help, but not many of them were wealthy. Joseph and Emma had very little to live on.

And now Emma was moving to Ohio, leaving her parents and relatives far behind, traveling to a place she had never seen. No home awaited her. She didn't even know how Joseph would make a living. Making things worse was the fact that she had been very sick all through December and was only now getting her strength back. The cold and the long days of travel would have been difficult for anyone, but Emma's pregnancy and recent illness made the trip a great hardship for her.

Each night for nearly a month the four travelers found lodging in public inns or with farmers. Although the journey was a real trial, Joseph and Emma felt they must go on. More than a hundred people had joined the Church in Kirtland, and the Lord had told the Saints to gather there. The Prophet had to lead the way.

On the first day of February Joseph stopped the sleigh in front of the Gilbert and Whitney store in Kirtland. Joseph marched into the store and spotted a man behind the counter. "Newel K. Whitney, thou art the man!" Joseph announced in a thundering voice, and he reached out to shake hands.

Newel Whitney was taken by surprise. "You have the

advantage of me," he said. "I could not call you by name as you have me."

Joseph grinned. "I am Joseph, the prophet. You have prayed me here, now what do you want of me?"

It was true. Newel Whitney *had* prayed that Joseph would come to Kirtland. Even before that, he and his wife, Elizabeth, had prayed for spiritual guidance. A voice had come to them, saying, "Prepare to receive the word of the Lord, for it is coming." Mormon missionaries had soon arrived in Kirtland and brought them the gospel, which they had accepted.

Joseph had seen Newel Whitney in a vision, kneeling and praying, and so Joseph had recognized him the instant that he stepped into the store. Brother Whitney already believed in the prophet, but now he saw firsthand that the man was blessed with special, visionary powers. He and his wife were honored to give Joseph and Emma a temporary place to live in their own home. But the house was crowded, and although Emma did the best she could in the cramped rooms, she worried about having enough space for a family.

A few weeks later, the Smiths were offered a one-room log cabin on land owned by Isaac Morley, another new Church member. It was a humble place, but again, Emma made the best she could of it. In this little home, on April 30th, she gave birth to twins, a girl and a boy.

But the babies were premature. They lived only about three hours.

Emma was heartbroken. She had now given birth to three children and had watched them all die within a few hours of their births. She felt terribly alone in this new place, away from her loved ones, housed in a tiny cabin, and robbed of the joy of children she had been expecting all through the hard winter. She was almost overwhelmed with grief.

Then a remarkable coincidence happened. On the very next day, a woman named Julia Murdock died while giving birth to twins—a boy and a girl. The babies needed a mother to nurse them or they would die. John Murdock, the father, took the babies to Emma to raise as her own. Emma was pained to think of Brother Murdock's great loss, but the babies brought her immediate joy.

The little cabin was suddenly filled with life again. But it was crowded, and it soon became a very busy place. Church members came to consult with Joseph, and investigators of the new church arrived at all hours of the day to meet the Prophet in person. Joseph found it difficult to do his work: compiling his revelations and preparing an inspired version of the Bible. Emma, along with raising the twins, was working on a hymnbook that the Lord had commanded her to prepare. She didn't even have a separate bedroom where she could let the babies sleep. The constant stream of visitors was a great burden.

One day Joseph and Emma were visited by a group of people from Hiram, Ohio, south of Kirtland: a couple named John and Elsa Johnson, a Methodist preacher named Ezra Booth, and some others who wished to learn more about the new religion. Elsa Johnson suffered with chronic rheumatism, which had left one of her arms almost useless. The guests asked many questions before one of them said to Joseph, "Here is Mrs. Johnson with a lame arm; has God given any power to man now on the earth to cure her?"

For a time Joseph said little. Later, when the subject had changed, he got up from his chair and walked to Elsa

Johnson. He took her arm in his hands and said, "Woman, in the name of the Lord Jesus Christ I command thee to be whole."

Elsa instantly raised her arm above her head—and everyone in the room knew that a miracle had just occurred. The next day, she was able to wash clothes without difficulty or pain.

The Johnsons were convinced that Joseph was a prophet. They soon joined the Church, as did Ezra Booth. Shortly afterward, John Johnson invited Joseph and Emma to move into the Johnsons' large farm home in Hiram, thirty-six miles from Kirtland. This was an answer to Joseph and Emma's prayers. They found comfort in this new home, which had enough living space and the peace and quiet they needed to carry out their work.

Throughout their lives, Joseph and Emma found little peace. Troubles and challenges always followed them—and would soon visit them in Hiram. But the winter of 1831–1832 was a sweet time, when the young couple found joy in the babies they had received as a gift, satisfaction in the work they were doing for the Lord, and the love of good friends who were willing to share their home.

For further reading, see Joseph Smith, History of the Church of Jesus Christ of Latter-day Saints, *ed. B. H. Roberts, 7 vols. (Salt Lake City: Deseret Book, 1951), 1:145–46; Milton V. Backman, Jr.,* The Heavens Resound *(Salt Lake City: Deseret Book, 1983), pp. 43–45.*

5

Lucy Smith Leads the Way to Kirtland

Joseph Smith has become known throughout the world as a powerful leader. This was no accident—he learned many things from the example of his parents. His mother, Lucy Mack Smith, was a particularly gifted leader. She was fearless and decisive, and she was ready to take on any challenge.

When the early Saints began to gather in Kirtland, Ohio, a group of members from Waterloo, New York, sold their farms and prepared to make the move. Some of those Saints were older than Lucy Smith, and several held the priesthood, but the entire group agreed that "Mother Smith" should be their leader.

She was a good choice.

The plan was for the eighty Saints to take a boat on the Erie Canal to Buffalo, and then to catch another boat across Lake Erie to Fairport, Ohio. From there, they would take wagons to Kirtland.

The group left New York in the early spring. The winter had been very cold, but the ice on the lake had supposedly broken up. As the Saints departed, a friend gave Lucy seventeen dollars to help buy food. As it turned out, she was glad she had the money.

Once they were on their way on the canal boat, Lucy called the group together to sing and pray. She then asked the fathers of the families whether they had enough supplies for the trip. She learned that most of them had very little. They had sold everything they had just to provide clothing, and were hoping that others in better circumstances might offer help. But few were in "better circumstances." Lucy had to use the seventeen dollars wisely, but she managed to feed those in need throughout the trip.

Lucy was disappointed with the way some of the mothers let their children run about on deck. There were many dangers on board. But the mothers told Lucy that their children simply wouldn't obey.

Lucy would hear none of that. She called the children together and told them, "When I come upstairs, and raise my hand, you must, every one of you, run to me as fast as you can." The children promised her they would do that. From that time on, when "Mother Smith" thought the children were getting too careless—or when the mothers weren't watching as well as they might—she merely raised her hand, the children came running, and order was restored.

When the boat was about halfway to Buffalo, the canal wall broke. The water fell to such a low level that the boat got stuck in the mud. Several of the men began to complain. They were certain they would be caught in the canal for a long time with no way to pay for the food they would need. They would surely starve.

Lucy listened to their complaints, and then she gave them this advice: Be patient and trust the Lord. She was certain He was looking out for them, whether it seemed like it or not. Chances were, the harbor in Buffalo was blocked with ice. If so, the Saints were better off on this canal boat than they would be seeking shelter in the crowded harbor town.

Two days later, the boat was moving again. When they finally got to Buffalo, the Saints learned that Lucy had been exactly right. The harbor was frozen over and was full of boats waiting but unable to sail.

While waiting in Buffalo, the Waterloo group learned that another group of Mormons, from Colesville, New York, had arrived ahead of them. They had been waiting for a week for the ice to break up so that they could cross the lake. Lucy asked the Colesville members whether they had told anyone about their religion. The Colesville Saints said they hadn't. They feared that no one would let Mormons rent a room or travel on a boat. They advised Lucy to keep quiet herself.

But Lucy wasn't about to hide the truth. "If you are ashamed of Christ," she told them, "you must not expect to be prospered; and I shall wonder if we do not get to Kirtland before you."

Lucy set out to find a boat to get her group across the lake. She knew a captain, and she sent some men to ask him for space on his vessel.

The men returned with good news. The boat was full, but the captain would let their party aboard if they didn't mind traveling on the open deck. It was the best they could hope for, so the Saints moved their belongings on board. But the ice was still holding, making it impossible to cross the lake. To make things worse, rain began to fall.

Several of the children in the group were sick. Lucy was concerned that if they stayed out in the cold and wet, everyone would fall ill. She sent one of the men into town to seek a warm, dry place to stay for the night. But when the man returned, he said that all the public houses were full. When the members heard that, they began to complain. Why hadn't they stayed at home until the weather was better? What would they do now?

Lucy had faith that she could find something. She headed for town herself.

At her first stop, the landlord said he would take the group in. But some guests complained that they didn't want to be crowded in with a lot of sick children. Lucy stiffened her back and said, "Never mind, it is no matter; I suppose I can get a room somewhere else, just as well."

At the next stop, she found someone who agreed to let the women and children stay—if Lucy would tell her all about this new religion she belonged to. Needless to say, Lucy was only too happy to do that.

The women and children got in out of the cold for the night, but the next morning the ship captain asked all to come on board again. He wanted to be able to leave at a moment's notice, if the ice broke up.

The Waterloo group was soon restless, and they began to complain once again. Lucy was tired of that, and she put a quick stop to it. She told the members, "Suppose that all the Saints here should lift up their hearts in prayer to God, that the way might be opened before us, how easy it would be for him to cause the ice to break away, so that in a moment we could be on our journey!"

At that moment, a man shouted from the shore, "Is the Book of Mormon true?"

He had asked the right person. Lucy bore him a powerful testimony of the book and of the church her son had helped restore to the earth. She then turned back and promised the members that if they would all pray to God for the ice to break, He would break it up for them.

They prayed. And the ice broke.

A crack in the ice stretched clear across the harbor. It was just wide enough for the boat to squeeze through. The captain set out immediately, and even though the boat was riding low in the water and people from the dock shouted that it would sink for sure, it stayed afloat and reached open water. Shortly after the boat cleared the harbor, the crack closed again. Lucy had been right. She would arrive in Kirtland well ahead of the Colesville Saints.

The passage was rough, and many of the Saints were seasick. Then, when they arrived in Fairport, some were worried because they couldn't afford to travel on to Kirtland. But Joseph Smith arrived to meet them. He had arranged for teams to transport the group the rest of the way. They made it to Kirtland safely.

"Mother Smith" had shown the strength that Joseph had known all his life. Lucy was a woman of faith, one who knew how to get a job done. No one in the Waterloo group would ever doubt that again.

For further reading, see Lucy Mack Smith, History of Joseph Smith, by His Mother *(Salt Lake City: Bookcraft, 1958), pp. 195–208.*

6

Parley's Great Escape

We think of the early Saints, especially the early missionaries, as serious, devoted people. And they were. But they also knew how to laugh. In fact, Parley P. Pratt, one of the greatest missionaries, had a wonderful sense of humor.

Parley had been a member of the Church for only a few weeks when Joseph Smith called him to serve a mission to the "western part of the United States," in what is now Missouri. Parley took just a few days to prepare and then set out.

Parley began his mission with Oliver Cowdery, Peter Whitmer, and Ziba Peterson. But the four missionaries had traveled only about fifty miles west of Kirtland, Ohio, when they ran into trouble. Some people in the area were violently opposed to what they called "Joe Smith's Golden Bible"—the Book of Mormon. These people were willing to do almost anything to silence the Mormon preachers.

One evening Parley and Ziba Peterson were teaching a man named Simeon Carter when a police officer barged in and arrested Parley. The officer took Parley down a dark, muddy road to appear before a judge that very night. Ziba went along too, although he was not under arrest himself.

Parley soon learned that the whole idea was to stop him from preaching. Even though the hour was late, a number of men had been brought in to make false charges. Parley decided not to defend himself against the lies. He remained absolutely silent.

The judge finally ordered Parley to pay a large fine or go to jail. Parley ignored the man. He asked Ziba to join him in singing a hymn, "O How Happy Are They."

The judge didn't think that was funny. He demanded that Parley pay the fine.

Parley had another solution. He proposed that the witnesses repent of their lies, and the judge repent of his injustice and abuse. If they would do that, and all kneel down with him, he would pray that God might forgive them of their sins.

The judge was not impressed with that offer either. He ordered a policeman, Officer Peabody, to take Parley off to jail.

The jail, however, was some miles off. For the first night, Parley was kept in a public inn. The next morning, while Parley and the police officer ate breakfast, the three other missionaries showed up. Parley whispered to them to go on without him. He would catch up soon.

He had a plan.

When Parley and the officer walked outside, Parley asked, "Mr. Peabody, are you good at a race?"

"No," the officer said, "but my big bull dog is." He added that the dog was trained to "take any man down," on command.

Parley didn't seem to worry about that. He smiled and thanked Officer Peabody for giving him "the chance to teach and sing" and for the night's lodging—with breakfast. Then he said, "I must now go on my journey; if you are good at a race you can accompany me. I thank you for all your kindness—good day, sir."

And Parley took off running.

The officer was stunned. He didn't move.

When Parley realized he wasn't being chased, he stopped and shouted to the officer again to join him in the race. But Mr. Peabody stood amazed, seemingly stuck to the ground.

Parley turned and ran again, and this time he increased his speed to "something like that of a deer." He was two hundred yards ahead before Mr. Peabody finally remembered to send the bulldog after him.

Parley had jumped a fence and was racing across a field toward the woods when the dog finally began to catch up. Mr. Peabody was running behind, pointing and shouting, "Stu-boy, stu-boy—take him—watch—lay hold of him, I say—down with him."

The dog was almost at Parley's heels, and Parley knew that he was about to lose the race, when the thought hit him that he should "assist the officer" in sending the dog on into the forest. Parley pointed to the woods and began shouting the same commands: "Take him down, boy. Lay hold of him."

The dog flew on past and kept right on going in the direction Parley was pointing. Parley ran on, yelling loudly to the dog, and Mr. Peabody followed, farther back, shouting for the dog to turn around. But the dog had a phantom to chase, and he wouldn't give up.

Parley made it to the woods and then doubled back and

slipped away. Before the day was over, he caught up with the other missionaries—with a very good story to tell.

The missionaries had a good laugh, and then they preached to a friendly audience that night. And meanwhile, Simeon Carter continued to study the Book of Mormon that the missionaries had left in his home. He became converted and traveled to Kirtland, where he was baptized and ordained an elder. When he returned home he preached the gospel and baptized nearly sixty people in the same place where Parley P. Pratt had fooled Mr. Peabody—and his dog.

For further reading, see Parley P. Pratt, Autobiography of Parley P. Pratt *(Salt Lake City: Deseret Book, 1975), pp. 48–51.*

7

An Attack on the Prophet

On a cold spring night in 1833, a mob of angry men learned a great deal about Joseph Smith. In fact, they may have learned more than they wanted to know.

While Joseph and Emma were living in Hiram, Ohio, some of the members of the Church in the area turned against the Prophet. Ezra Booth began to publish letters containing all sorts of accusations, and Symonds Ryder had become an open enemy to both Joseph and the Church.

The two former believers claimed that Joseph Smith and Sidney Rigdon wanted to take away the Church members' land to make themselves rich. Joseph taught that all the Saints should share what they had, not that any *one* person would come out better than the rest. But some people didn't understand that. Symonds Ryder was also bothered by Joseph's tendency to laugh and joke, which he didn't think a prophet should do.

These and other complaints were spread through the area, along with lies about the teachings of the Church. A number of men, roused by the charges—and by whiskey—decided to attack the Prophet and try to drive him away.

At the time, Joseph and Emma were nursing their adopted

twins, who were sick with measles. On Saturday night, March 24, Emma had gone to bed with little Julia by her side. Joseph had lain down near her, in the trundle bed, with baby Joseph next to him. Emma heard a tapping on the window but thought nothing of it.

Suddenly a mob of men burst into the house. They forced their way into the bedroom, which was near the front door. The men grabbed the Prophet by his hair and bedclothes and dragged him outside. Fighting hard, Joseph was able to free a leg and kick a man hard enough to knock him down and bloody his nose. But powerful as he was, Joseph didn't have a chance. A mob of forty or fifty men were waiting to get their hands on the man they hated.

While several men held Joseph, the man with the bloody nose grabbed him by the neck and choked him until he passed out. When Joseph came to, men were carrying him away from the house and into a field. He spotted Sidney Rigdon lying unconscious on the ground. He thought the mob had killed poor Sidney, and he expected the same for himself. But when he asked the men to spare his life, one of them said, "Call on yer God for help, we'll show ye no mercy."

They carried him farther from the house and then tore off his clothes and beat him. One man fell on him like a mad cat, ripped his skin with his fingernails, and growled, "That's the way the Holy Ghost falls on folks."

Some of the men shouted threats on Joseph's life. Others threatened to mutilate his body. Joseph tried to fight the men off, but he was held securely. He felt hot tar being poured on his body and face. One man tried to push the tar paddle into his mouth, and another pushed a small bottle against his teeth, claiming it was full of poison. Joseph resisted and the bottle broke, chipping one of his teeth at the same time.

The men threw feathers over him, which stuck in the tar, and then they scattered, leaving him on the cold ground. Joseph rested for a few minutes and got his breath as best he could. He collapsed the first time he tried to stand up, but he struggled to his feet again and cleared the tar from his lips so he could breathe better. Then he staggered back to the house.

Emma saw him coming. In the darkness, she thought the tar on his body was blood, and she fainted. Friends had gathered by now. They wrapped Joseph in a blanket and took him inside. The long, painful process of scraping away the tar took all night.

The next morning was Sunday, and Joseph was scheduled to preach a sermon. He dressed himself, in spite of the concern of Emma and his friends, and kept his appointment. He preached the sermon he had prepared even though his face was scraped and bruised and he was still exhausted from the long night's agony.

Some of the mob from the night before had come to hear what Joseph would say. But he made no mention of what had happened, and he expressed no bitterness or anger. He simply preached the gospel of Jesus Christ, astounding all who listened.

That afternoon Joseph baptized three new members. And later, some of the men from the mob, having seen the Prophet's noble behavior in the face of such cruelty, joined the Church.

For further reading, see Joseph Smith, History of The Church of Jesus Christ of Latter-day Saints, *ed. B. H. Roberts, 7 vols. (Salt Lake City: Deseret Book, 1951), 1:259–65; Lucy Mack Smith,* History of Joseph Smith, by His Mother *(Salt Lake City: Bookcraft, 1958), pp. 218–21; Donna Hill,* Joseph Smith, the First Mormon *(New York: Doubleday, 1977), pp. 218–21.*

8

Tar and Feathers

While Joseph Smith was in Kirtland, Ohio, he wanted to find another place, farther to the west, where more Saints could gather and build a center for the Church. The place chosen was near Independence, Jackson County, Missouri. Church members began to locate there in 1832.

But troubles soon developed. Most of the old Missouri settlers were from southern states where slavery was practiced. The Saints were nearly all from the northeast, and they were opposed to slavery. The old settlers feared that the balance of power in the county would shift. The Mormons, who seemed overly religious and strange to the old settlers, were coming in large numbers. They could take over the county and press their attitudes against slavery.

In the summer of 1833, a large group of the old settlers held a meeting in Independence. The meeting was supposed to be an orderly discussion of ways to get rid of the Mormons. But many of the men were drunk and unreasonable. They were ready for a fight.

The old settlers agreed that the Mormons should leave the county. The majority of them voted to give the Saints time to get things organized and move out peacefully. But that didn't satisfy the anger of many in the group, and they turned into a mob. As the meeting broke up, nearly three hundred men, wild with anger, headed for the Mormon newspaper office where William Phelps published *The Evening and the Morning Star*. They shoved the printing press out the second-story window. When they found copies of the *Book of Commandments*—the first publication of Joseph Smith's revelations—they scattered the pages in the streets.

The mob also tore up a Mormon-owned store, and then they went looking for the bishop. Edward Partridge, the first bishop of the Church, was the highest Mormon authority in Jackson County, so the mob chose him as their target.

Bishop Partridge was sitting with his wife, who had recently had a baby. Three men barged in the door and dragged the bishop outside. Then they put him on a horse and rode away with him.

The bishop's daughters, Emily and Eliza, had gone to a nearby spring for water. They saw about fifty men surround their house and drag their father outside. They hid and watched as the mob disappeared with their father. Then the girls ran to their mother in the house. They were terrified that their father was about to be murdered.

Edward Partridge was taken to the town square, where the rest of the mob was waiting. He and another Mormon man named Charles Allen were quickly surrounded. Russel Hicks, one of the leaders of the mob, warned the bishop and Brother Allen that they and the rest of the Saints would have to deny the Book of Mormon or leave the county. If they refused, they would be driven out.

Given the chance to speak, Bishop Partridge answered calmly. He told the men that Saints had suffered persecution in all ages of the world. He had done nothing to offend any of these people. If they abused him, they would be abusing an innocent man. "I am willing to suffer for the sake of Christ," he told them, but he refused to leave the county.

The bishop's speech only made the crowd angrier. They pressed in around him and Charles Allen, screaming and jeering, cursing and swearing. Some of them shouted, "Call on your Jesus!" Others wanted to hear what Bishop Partridge was saying, and they shouted for quiet.

Everything was out of control, and Edward Partridge had no idea what the mob intended to do. But he remained calm as they knocked him down and kicked him. They tore away his coat and hat and vest, and they began to strip away his other clothes. "Would you leave me here naked in the street?" he cried.

For some reason, they responded to this, leaving his pants and shirt on. But they covered him from head to foot with tar, and they poured feathers over him. Then they did the same to Charles Allen.

The crowd continued to taunt and shout insults. But slowly, as the men watched the quiet, dignified way that the bishop accepted their treatment, the noise began to die down. The mob watched as the bishop rose to his feet. He was a tall, straight man, and even in the tar and feathers, he looked dignified. The men had meant to shame him; instead, they were the ones feeling the shame. The entire crowd had fallen silent.

Bishop Partridge kept his quiet composure as the circle opened and the mob let him walk away. Charles Allen followed. The men of the mob seemed to recognize that they had faced better men than themselves—and lost to their meekness.

For further reading, see Donna Hill, Joseph Smith, the First Mormon *(New York: Doubleday, 1977), pp. 160–62; Parley P. Pratt,* The Autobiography of Parley P. Pratt *(Salt Lake City: Deseret Book, 1975), p. 191.*

9

Philo Dibble's Miraculous Recovery

In the autumn of 1833, the old settlers of Jackson County, Missouri, got bolder about attacking the Mormon settlements. Night riders pulled down or burned log homes. They ran off cattle and trampled crops, and they severely beat a number of the Mormon men.

The Saints were angry that a mob, by brute force, could steal away their land—their Zion. At first, even though the Mormons were greatly outnumbered, they stood their ground. Finally, when armed men attacked a small troop of Saints, the Mormons fought back.

The battle didn't last long, but when it was over Andrew Barber, a Mormon, lay dying, and two of the old settlers were dead. A number of men from both sides were wounded. One of them was a Mormon named Philo Dibble.

Philo was "gutshot"—wounded in the abdomen—and was as good as dead. Surgery of the abdomen was impossible in those days. If a man wounded this way didn't bleed to death, infection would kill him.

What made things worse was that the reign of terror had spread, and the Saints were fleeing from the county. Most were piling their belongings into wagons and heading toward

the Missouri River to cross into Clay County. Others, forced from their homes in the cold and rain, were walking, taking nothing more than the clothes on their backs. One group headed south. Snow covered the heavy prairie grass that had burned that fall. The stubbly grass cut the feet of the children, many of whom had no shoes. Rescuers later tracked the group by following the blood on the snow.

Friends of Philo Dibble had a tough choice to make. No one wanted to leave him behind, but there seemed to be no way to save him, and if they stayed with him in the county, they would be in great danger. One man, Newel Knight, refused to give up. He risked his life to get to the Dibble home. Slipping past the mob, he entered the home, quickly gave his friend a priesthood blessing, and then rode away.

The next day, as Newel Knight was leaving the county, he met up with none other than Philo Dibble—ten miles from where he had given him the blessing the day before. Philo was actually well enough to have joined the fleeing Saints. He told Newel that as soon as he had received the blessing, the pain seemed to move as though a "power were driving it," and in a few minutes it was gone. Then his body discharged a large amount of infected fluid, along with the bullet and even some cloth from his shirt.

Philo Dibble made it safely into Clay County, and he recovered completely. After surviving further trials in Missouri and Illinois, he crossed the plains to Utah. He served the Church in many callings throughout the rest of his long life.

For further reading, see Parley P. Pratt, Autobiography of Parley P. Pratt *(Salt Lake City: Deseret Book, 1975), pp. 99–100;* Joseph Smith, History of The Church of Jesus Christ of Latter-day Saints, *ed. B. H. Roberts, 7 vols. (Salt Lake City: Deseret Book, 1951), 1:431.*

10

George A. Smith and Zion's Camp

In the summer of 1834, the Saints who had been driven out of Jackson County by the old settlers were living in Clay County. Many found shelter in barns or sheds or abandoned cabins, and were scraping along the best they could. They still hoped to return across the river to their homes. Governor Daniel Dunklin had promised to help them return if they could organize their own army to protect themselves.

In Kirtland, Ohio, where a large number of Saints still lived, Joseph Smith received a revelation that he should create a little army to aid the scattered Saints. Just over two hundred men agreed to serve. They planned to march a thousand miles to Missouri and help their brothers and sisters return to Jackson County, the place they called Zion.

George A. Smith felt honored when he was invited to travel with the militia that would be called Zion's Camp. At sixteen, he would be the youngest soldier to make the long march. George A., who was Joseph Smith's cousin, was even more thrilled when the Prophet invited him to sleep in the same tent and serve as Joseph's personal guard.

George A. was a big, awkward boy with poor eyesight. He wanted to serve the Prophet well, but he had very little confidence in himself. Comparing himself to Joseph, who was such a great leader and speaker, he didn't think he was very talented.

And in truth, anyone who had seen George A. at that time might have thought him a rather sorry sight. His parents had given up almost everything they owned to gather with the Saints to Ohio. They were left with little money to outfit their son for the march. George's mother made him a pair of pants out of striped mattress cloth and a backpack from checked apron fabric. His father gave him a new pair of boots and an old musket left over from the Revolutionary War.

George A. reported that after a few days of walking, his new boots had worn bloody blisters on his feet, so that every step he took was painful. He had also ripped his pants to shreds, and he had sat on his straw hat, smashing it into a shape like a bird's nest.

What a warrior!

Besides comparing himself to the Prophet, George A. also compared himself to another of his cousins, Jesse Smith, who was also a member of the camp. Jesse was a little older, and he had more of the dash and personality of their older cousin Joseph. Still, George A. tried to make himself valuable in all the ways he could. He kept a careful record in his journal of all that happened. Because he spent his days with the Prophet, he knew most of what was going on.

George A. was also loyal to Joseph when other men turned against him. Times got very hard, and it's no wonder that some of the men became discouraged. They marched twenty-five to forty miles each day and then could hardly sleep during the hot, muggy nights. Mosquitoes and flies made life miserable, and food was in short supply. The men lived mostly on fried cornmeal mush (called corn dodgers) or on fried bread. The meat they carried with them began to rot, but the men trimmed off the worst of the spoiled parts and ate it anyway. George A. said the water they found on the prairie was usually filled with "living creatures," but he learned to strain the "wigglers" with his teeth as he drank.

One of the brethren, a man named Sylvester Smith, got tired of the conditions and complained bitterly to the Prophet. Sylvester was "strong-willed and sharp-tongued." His nasty attitude threatened to destroy the spirit of the entire group. Joseph told him and some other rebellious brethren that if they didn't repent and show more loyalty, serious trials would come on the camp that very night. The next morning, most of the pack horses were so lame that they could barely be led to water.

The Prophet asked all the men to humble themselves. He promised that if they would, the horses would be made well. By noon, all but one of the horses was ready to move on. Sylvester Smith's horse had died.

George A. watched all this and learned. Young as he was, he tried to do everything he could to support the Prophet.

As the camp reached Missouri, the situation became tense. Joseph learned that Governor Dunklin had changed his mind and had withdrawn his support. War might be ahead, and the outcome didn't look good. The Saints, even with Zion's Camp for support, would be greatly outnumbered.

The camp was spared from fighting any battles. But the long march ended in frustration. Attempts to buy the land in Jackson County or to work out some compromise failed. The Saints had avoided a war, but they were not able to return to Zion. Joseph Smith received a revelation that the time for that return would have to wait. Part of the reason was that the Saints in Jackson County had not lived up to all their commitments to the Lord—and to each other.

Most of the members of Zion's Camp, though they were disappointed, accepted the word of the Lord. They began to organize for the march back to Ohio. But some were bitter. They accused Joseph Smith of leading them on a pointless, miserable trek. They claimed he was no prophet.

Joseph, humbled and disappointed himself, told the men that if they continued in their rebellion, he feared that a terrible fate would come upon the entire company. A few days later the members of Zion's Camp began to fall ill with cholera. Sixty-eight were stricken, and fourteen died.

Among the dead was Jesse Smith.

Joseph was heartbroken at the loss of such a fine young man, and George A. simply could not understand why it had to happen. He told the Prophet, "The Lord should have taken me instead." George A. was certain that he would never be the man that Jesse might have become, that he would never serve the Church half as well.

And so, it seemed, Zion's Camp had turned out to be a long, frustrating march that accomplished nothing except to kill a few of its members and drive a few more away from the Church.

But in the next few years, the value of the march began to be clear. Those who remained loyal, who learned leadership, who gained strength, became the leaders of the Church. Nine of the members of the first Quorum of the Twelve Apostles and all of the members of the original Quorum of the Seventy were chosen from men who had made the march and stayed true. Brigham Young, who would later become the leader of the Church, said that he wouldn't trade all the wealth in his county for what he had learned from his experience with Zion's Camp.

And what about George A. Smith, the awkward boy who thought he should have died in place of his cousin Jesse? Less than five years later, at the age of twenty-one, he was ordained an apostle. He later served with Brigham Young as a member of the First Presidency of the Church. His experience in Zion's Camp prepared him for a lifetime of leadership. His only mistake had been to underestimate his potential greatness.

For further reading, see Merlo J. Pusey, Builders of the Kingdom *(Provo, Utah: Brigham Young University Press, 1981), pp. 9–18; Milton V. Backman, Jr.,* The Heavens Resound *(Salt Lake City: Deseret Book, 1983), pp. 179–95; Joseph Smith,* History of The Church of Jesus Christ of Latter-day Saints, *ed. B. H. Roberts, 7 vols. (Salt Lake City: Deseret Book, 1951), 2:61–134.*

11

Saved by a Storm

The men of Zion's Camp were tested to the limit. Some were not up to the test, but the majority never doubted that God was with them. On several occasions the men were protected from their enemies. One night in particular, when an army of Missouri old settlers had threatened to attack and destroy the camp, even the forces of nature came to the rescue.

By June 19, 1834, Zion's Camp had crossed most of Missouri. As the marchers neared Clay County, they began to receive warnings that an attack was coming.

That night the men set up their camp on a section of high ground between the Big Fishing River and the Little Fishing River. Anyone who attacked them would have to cross one of those rivers. When the army had crossed the Little Fishing River that afternoon, however, the water hadn't been even as high as their boot tops, and the weather was calm.

As the Saints were setting up their tents for the night, five men wearing guns rode into camp. They announced that nearly four hundred men, gathered from the surrounding counties, were ready to attack. They promised to kill every member of Zion's Camp.

Wilford Woodruff wrote that when the men rode away, the sky was blue. But shortly after, he noticed a small, dark cloud that began to "unroll itself like a scroll" across the sky. In a few minutes the heavens were black, and then rain began to fall. A wild, intense storm followed.

Parley Pratt said it was the kind of storm "seldom witnessed on our earth." Rain fell in torrents and thunder crashed and rumbled. Joseph Smith said the lightning was so constant that throughout the night he could see everything around him in perfect detail.

The men in the camp spent a frightening night in the rain and mud. Joseph and George A. Smith dug a trench around their tent, but the inside still filled up with six inches of water. George A. finally climbed out of the tent and dropped, exhausted, into the back of a wagon and slept in the driving rain. Some of the men took cover in an old log church. Others managed the best they could in their flooded tents, which were whipped and sometimes even torn away by the raging winds.

But the men, wet and cold as they were, survived the night. In the morning they tested their guns—and almost all of them fired. All was well, and the storm had passed over them. The skies were now clear.

Meanwhile, however, their attackers had not come out of the storm so well. The Little Fishing River, which the men of Zion's Camp had walked through the day before, was now thirty feet deep. The Big Fishing River was even deeper. Both were too dangerous to cross. The Saints had been protected from the planned attack.

About forty men from the mob had crossed the Missouri River from Jackson County as the storm had begun. Many more had planned to follow. But the first group was pinned down all night by hailstones the size of eggs. The wind tore trees up by their roots, and the furious hail broke away limbs. The hailstones actually broke the stocks of some of the men's rifles.

One Jackson County man was killed by lightning. Another had his hand torn off as he tried to hold his bolting horse. The rain, hail, and floods kept the rest of the mob from even crossing the Missouri River into Clay County.

After a terrifying night under wagons, in hollow logs, or anywhere the old settlers could protect themselves, they were humbled and frightened. Besides, their ammunition was soaked and wouldn't fire. And so they boarded their boat and rowed back across the Missouri River. Some had lost their horses, which had been run off by the storm. Not one had the heart to consider trying another assault on Zion's Camp.

At the very height of the storm, when some of the men of Zion's Camp had complained, Joseph told them, "Boys, there is some meaning to this. God is in this storm." And he was not the only one who thought so. When the old settlers learned that the Saints had only been rained on, while they, just a few miles away, had been pounded by hail, some of them said that if God fought for the Mormons that way, "we might as well go about [our] business."

And that's just what they did.

For further reading, see Merlo J. Pusey, Builders of the Kingdom *(Provo, Utah: Brigham Young University Press, 1981), pp. 14–15; Parley P. Pratt,* Autobiography of Parley P. Pratt *(Salt Lake City: Deseret Book, 1975), p. 116.*

12

Sarah's Dream

In 1835, at the age of twenty, Sarah Pea heard about the restored gospel for the first time. Her father happened to meet two Mormon missionaries, and he invited them to his home in St. Clair County, near Bellville, Illinois. The missionaries explained the first principles of the gospel, and they told the Pea family about the Book of Mormon.

The meeting ended late in the afternoon, so Mr. Pea invited the missionaries to spend the night. After supper, many of the Peas' neighbors came over to hear the two strangers preach. Sarah was fascinated with what she heard. She asked to see a copy of the Book of Mormon. She left the other guests, took the book to her room, and read it throughout the evening and much of the night. It left a strong impression on her.

The missionaries were on their way to Kirtland, Ohio—five hundred miles away—so they left the next morning. Sarah and her family continued to think about what they had heard. They thought, however, that they would never see the elders again.

And then, six weeks later, Sarah announced that the missionaries were coming back.

Sarah had dreamed on a Friday night that the two elders would arrive at their home the following evening at sundown. In the dream, they stepped onto her porch and said certain words that she remembered specifically.

The morning after her dream, Sarah warned her parents, who were going to town, to hurry home in time to meet the Mormon missionaries. They just laughed at her. Sarah also told her sister about her dream, but her sister laughed too.

All day, Sarah and her sister cooked and got ready for Sunday. As the afternoon and evening wore on, Sarah began to watch out the door for the elders.

As the sun was setting the missionaries appeared, exactly as it had happened in her dream. When they stepped onto her porch, the conversation that followed was word for word what she remembered from her dream:

> "I have been looking for you to come," she said.
>
> "Why, had you heard we were coming?"
>
> "No, I dreamed last night that you would come, and I felt sure you would be here."
>
> "Well," said one of the missionaries, "we had a dream that we were to return here and baptize you and build up a church in this region."
>
> "Well," responded Sarah, "that is something for the future."

Not much later, Sarah's parents returned. Her father laughed and said, "Well, Sarah, where are your Mormon elders?" Just then the elders stepped out onto the porch. Mr. and Mrs. Pea were astounded!

But Sarah and her family were soon baptized.

The Peas eventually moved to Far West, Missouri, where Sarah met and married Charles Coulson Rich. She and her husband were driven by mobs from their homes in Missouri and in Nauvoo, Illinois. They eventually crossed the plains to Utah. They raised a fine family and Brother Rich was called as an apostle of the Lord. With her husband, Sarah served as a leader in founding settlements in San Bernardino, California, and in Bear Lake Valley on the Utah-Idaho border.

Sarah had learned at an early age to trust in the Lord's guidance, and she never lost that trust.

For further reading, see John Henry Evans, Charles Coulson Rich *(New York: Macmillan, 1936), pp. 38–40.*

13

A Fight at the Gallatin Election

The Saints who were driven from Jackson County remained in Clay County for more than a year. Some began to see the area as a place to gather until they could move back into Jackson County. But Clay County citizens, sympathetic at first, became alarmed about so many Mormons moving in. The Saints knew they would have to move on again, and so they worked out an agreement with officials of the state of Missouri to settle in two counties where fewer people lived. These were Caldwell and Daviess counties, in the northern part of the state. There, the Saints gathered again and built the settlements of Far West and Adam-Ondi-Ahman.

But the same old problems soon returned. As the members began to move to Missouri from Kirtland, Ohio, the number of Mormons in Caldwell and Daviess counties grew to more than five thousand, with more coming. The old settlers in the area didn't want their counties to be dominated by a group of outsiders, especially these rather strange newcomers. But this time the Saints were tired of being driven away. This was America, and they had a right to live where

they chose. They decided to stand their ground—even to fight if they had to.

On August 8, 1838, an election was held in the town of Gallatin. Two weeks before the election, a non-Mormon judge who was friendly to the Church warned that the old settlers might try to keep the Saints from voting. He told the Mormon men to go to the elections armed and prepared to protect themselves (in 1838 women did not have the right to vote). The Saints, however, ignored the warning and arrived at the elections unarmed.

A man named William P. Peniston, who had been an enemy of the Saints in Clay County, was running for the state legislature. In recent weeks he had tried to gain the Mormon vote by pretending he was a friend after all. But that plan hadn't worked, and now he was afraid that if the Mormons got to vote, they would keep him from winning.

Peniston served up plenty of whiskey to a rough bunch of old settlers, and then he stood on a barrel and gave a speech. He told the crowd that if the Mormons voted, they would seize control of the county and prevent the old settlers from voting in the future.

The Mormons, he said, were horse thieves, liars, and counterfeiters. "They profess to heal the sick, and cast out devils," he shouted, "and you all know that is a lie."

When a small group of Mormons approached the balloting place, a drunken man named Richard Weldon stopped an elderly man named Samuel Brown. "Are you a Mormon preacher?" he demanded. Samuel Brown said that he was. "Do you Mormons believe in healing the sick by the laying on of hands, speaking [in] tongues, and casting out devils?"

Once again, Brother Brown said yes. Mr. Weldon shouted that Brown was a liar, and then he began to beat the old man.

Another Mormon, Hyrum Nelson, stepped in to stop the beating and took some hard blows himself from several of the old settlers. The other Mormons in the group weren't going to stand by and watch this. Riley Stewart picked up a good-sized stick and gave Richard Weldon a solid blow over the head.

Weldon dropped to the ground, and suddenly everyone got into the fight. One of the old settlers pulled a knife and tried to stab Riley Stewart. But a Mormon by the name of John Butler had grabbed a solid stick of oak. Just as the old settler stuck Riley Stewart's shoulder with his knife, John Butler hit the old settler over the head with his stick.

The Mormon men were badly outnumbered, maybe ten to one, but they fought like lions. One of the old settlers, who took a blow in the face with a two-pound rock, called out that he had never seen people hit as hard as the Mormons did.

John Butler later wrote a report on the whole incident. He said that one Mormon, Brother Olmstead, had bought some earthenware bowls and dishes that day. He had wrapped them up in a cotton handkerchief in order to carry them home on horseback. When he was surrounded and had to fight, he used the dishes as a weapon, and he used them well. When the fight was over, the dishes were broken into a thousand pieces, no piece bigger than a silver dollar, and the handkerchief "looked as though cows had been chewing on it." But Brother Olmstead was still feeling fine. The same could not be said of some of those who had gotten in his way.

John Butler wrote that he didn't want to kill anyone, only

to protect himself and his brothers. "When I got in reach," he said, "I commenced to call out loud for peace." But at the same time, he continued to swing his stick. He said he thought he was only "tapping" his enemies lightly, but they dropped to the ground, one after the other, as though they were dead.

Most who saw the incident agreed that the dozen or so Mormons not only held their own but won the fight. No one recorded, though, how many were actually able to vote.

In the next few days, the story spread through the state that Mormons had attacked a group of old settlers in Gallatin. Things got worse from that point. Mormons were accused of every sort of bad behavior. But they had only fought because they wanted to vote. And then, under attack, they had stood together and protected each other.

John Butler couldn't help it if his little "taps" had turned out the lights on so many of the old settlers!

For further reading, see Joseph Smith, History of The Church of Jesus Christ of Latter-day Saints, *ed. B. H. Roberts, 7 vols. (Salt Lake City, Deseret Book, 1951), 3:56–58; Donna Hill,* Joseph Smith, the First Mormon *(New York: Doubleday, 1977), pp. 228–30.*

14

Haun's Mill—A Massacre and a Miracle

Far West and Adam-Ondi-Ahman were the largest of the Mormon communities in northern Missouri. Many Mormons in the area lived in tiny settlements. One of those was Haun's Mill, where about thirty families lived. The Prophet Joseph had advised them to move to the larger communities for safety, but they chose to stay where they were. Several of them had just arrived from Ohio and were still living in tents or wagons. It was at Haun's Mill that one of the greatest trials came to the early Saints.

In 1838, the governor of Missouri, Lilburn W. Boggs, listened to lies and rumors and finally sided with the old settlers of Caldwell and Daviess counties, who wanted to get rid of all Mormons. He issued a written statement that said, among other things, "The Mormons must be treated as enemies and must be exterminated or driven from the state."

"Extermination" is something done to cockroaches or termites, not to human beings. But the order was taken to be a license to kill, and some of the old settlers acted immediately.

On Tuesday, October 30, late in the afternoon, 240 armed men of the Missouri state militia rode their horses toward Haun's Mill. Children were outside playing, and men and women were working in the fields, harvesting crops. A few of the Mormon men were standing guard, however, worried that just such an attack might happen. When the guards saw the large group of armed men, riding hard and looking angry, they put down their guns, waved their hats, and called for peace. The mob answered by firing their first shots.

The old settlers charged into the settlement, shouting and swearing and shooting. A few of the Mormon men tried to return the gunfire, but others, seeing no hope, scattered and tried to hide. One of the mob leaders shouted, "Shoot everything with breeches, and shoot to kill!"

The men listened only to the order to kill. They shot at the women and children who were running to the woods for protection. Amanda Smith, a Mormon woman, grabbed her two little daughters and hurried across a plank over the mill pond. As she ran into the woods, bullets flew around her, tearing through her clothes. Another sister, Mary Stedwell, who was running alongside Amanda, was struck by a bullet and fell. Amanda helped her get behind a log and told her to stay down.

As Mary huddled against the ground, the mobbers shot at her dress, which was draped over the log. They apparently thought they were hitting her, finishing her off. More than twenty bullets were later cut from the log.

A number of the Mormon men and boys ran into the blacksmith's shop with the hope of using it as a fort. It was a log building, but there were wide gaps between the logs. Those inside were caught like animals in a cage. The mob surrounded the shop and fired through the gaps. Eight of those inside were killed. Some, who ran from the shop, were able to get away, although several were wounded. Others were killed as they tried to make their escape.

Warren Smith, Amanda's husband, and his sons Sardius and Alma were among those in the blacksmith's shop. Warren was killed. Sardius, who was ten years old, managed to slide under the blacksmith's bellows, where he tried to hide. But the men of the mob found him and dragged him outside, where they put a gun to his head and shot him.

Once the shooting was over, and all the Mormon men were dead or wounded or had managed to get away, the mob looted the houses. They even stole the boots and clothes off some of the bodies. One man rode off with a bonnet that he said he wanted for his sweetheart.

When the mob cleared out, some of the Mormons came out of hiding to discover the horror. Of the thirty or so men in the settlement, fifteen were dead, along with two boys. A few other men died later. Several others, both men and women, were wounded, some of them disabled for life.

When Amanda Smith came out of hiding, she saw her oldest son carrying one of his younger brothers out of the shop. "Oh! My Alma is dead!" she cried. Seven-year-old Alma was actually still alive, though badly wounded in the hip. But her husband and Sardius were dead.

Amanda later wrote that in spite of her grief, she couldn't cry. Her "mother's sense" focused all her attention on Alma, who seemed to have little hope of surviving. One of the members of the mob had stuck his rifle through a crack in the logs of the blacksmith shop, placed the barrel against the boy's hip, and fired. Not only the flesh but the hip bone itself had been shot away. Sister Smith wrote:

We laid little Alma on a bed in our tent and examined the wound. It was a ghastly sight. I knew not what to do. . . .

The women were sobbing, in the greatest anguish of spirit; the children were crying loudly with fear and grief at the loss of fathers and brothers; the dogs howled over their dead masters and the cattle were terrified with the scent of the blood of the murdered.

Yet I was there, all that long, dreadful night, with my dead and my wounded, and none but God as our physician and help.

"Oh my Heavenly Father," I cried, "what shall I do? Thou seest my poor wounded boy and knowest my inexperience. Oh Heavenly Father, direct me what to do!"

And then I was directed as by a voice speaking to me.

The voice told Sister Smith to make medicines from the ashes of the fire and from the root of a slippery elm tree. Then she was directed to wash and bandage the wound. All the while she talked to her son:

"Alma, my child!" I said, "you believe that the Lord made your hip?"

"Yes, mother."

"Well, the Lord can make something there in the place of your hip, don't you believe he can, Alma?"

"Do you think that the Lord can, mother?"
inquired the child, in his simplicity.

"Yes, my son," I replied, "he has shown it all
to me in a vision."

Then I laid him comfortably on his face, and
said: "Now you lay like that, and don't move,
and the Lord will make you another hip."

Some of the Saints, in the face of such violence, simply
gave up. They left the Church or returned to their former
homes, away from the rest of the Saints. But most did not.
Most of them found ways to survive, ways to discover
strengths they didn't know they possessed. Amanda Smith
was one of those survivors. She had lost a husband and a son,
but she hadn't lost her faith.

She later described the miracle that came five weeks after
the Haun's Mill massacre:

I was out of the house fetching a bucket of
water, when I heard screams from the children.
Running back, in affright, I entered, and there
was Alma on the floor, dancing around, and the
children screaming in astonishment and joy.

It is now nearly forty years ago, but Alma has
never been the least crippled during his life, and
he has traveled quite a long period of the time
as a missionary of the gospel and a living
miracle of the power of God.

Mormons, it would appear, are not all that easy to exter-
minate.

For further reading, see Leonard J. Arrington and Davis Bitton, The Mormon Experience *(New York: Knopf, 1979), p. 45; Edward W. Tullidge,* The Women of Mormondom *(New York, 1877), pp. 475–77.*

15

Alexander Doniphan: Friend to the Saints

The same day the massacre occurred at Haun's Mill—October 30, 1838—leaders at Far West received warnings that more than two thousand Missouri soldiers were marching toward their city. The Saints prepared themselves for an all-out fight. They built barricades for protection by tearing down log cabins and turning wagons on their sides.

The first army to arrive was headed by General Samuel D. Lucas from Jackson County, a longtime enemy of the Saints. Joseph Smith led a small group of men on a spying mission that night. He came away satisfied that General Lucas's army was setting up camp and would not yet attack. But no one knew what the next morning might bring.

During the night many of the soldiers rode onto Mormon farms. They trampled crops and killed animals. One soldier used the butt of his rifle to bash a Mormon man in the head. He claimed that the man, called only "Brother Carey" in later reports, had burned the soldier's house. When Sister Carey tried to help her husband, soldiers stopped her. She could only watch as her husband bled to death. Later,

Mormons learned that the soldier's house had not, in fact, been burned.

The next morning the men of Far West took up their positions at the barricades. But news came that Governor Boggs had sent Major General John Clark with several thousand more troops to carry out the destruction of their city. The Saints would be overwhelmingly outnumbered.

General Lucas, early in the day, led his troops toward Far West, but when he saw that the Mormons were armed and ready, he retreated. A stand-off lasted through most of the day. Finally, Lucas approached the town again, this time with 250 soldiers under a white flag of truce. He demanded that the Mormons give up their guns and turn over their leaders to the army.

The Saints had hoped to hold their ground, appeal for justice, and somehow find a way to keep their homes. But Joseph Smith could now see that a bloodbath was coming. He asked Colonel George Hinkle, the highest ranking military leader in the Far West militia, to go out and negotiate with General Lucas.

When Hinkle returned, he told Joseph that General Lucas wanted to hold a council with the Mormon leaders. Perhaps an agreement could be worked out that would save the lives of the people. Joseph took Parley Pratt, Sidney Rigdon, and a few other Church leaders and rode out to hold the council. But as the Mormon leaders approached the waiting soldiers, General Lucas commanded his men to grab and arrest them.

Many of the soldiers had painted themselves with Indian-style war paint. And many were drunk. As they grabbed the Mormon leaders, they shouted with a terrifying, eerie howl that everyone in Far West could hear. Every Saint shuddered to think what now might happen to their beloved Prophet.

Joseph and the others were forced to spend the whole night in the open while a hard rain fell. As they lay in the mud, their enemies held a court to decide their fate. The Mormon leaders were not allowed to speak on their own behalf.

While the so-called court continued, guards taunted Joseph. "Come, Mr. Smith, show us an angel," they demanded.

Late in the night, the court reached a decision. Lucas sent the following order to Brigadier-General Alexander Doniphan, the commanding officer of one of the armies under Lucas's command:

> Sir: You will take Joseph Smith and the other prisoners into the public square at Far West and shoot them at 9 o'clock tomorrow morning.
> Samuel D. Lucas, Major-General Commanding.

General Doniphan, besides being a militia commander, was an attorney. He and his partners had once been hired by Joseph Smith to represent the Church during the negotiations when the Saints had been driven out of Jackson County. General Doniphan knew Joseph well, and he admired him. As a military officer, his obligation was to carry out the order. On the other hand, as a decent human being who believed in justice, he knew that what Lucas was commanding him to do was deeply wrong.

He didn't hesitate. He quickly sent a note back to Lucas:

It is cold-blooded murder. I will not obey your order. My brigade shall march for Liberty tomorrow morning, at 8 o'clock; and if you execute these men, I will hold you responsible before an earthly tribunal, so help me God.

A. W. Doniphan, Brigadier-General.

General Doniphan kept his promise. In the morning he marched his troops away from Far West. Now Lucas was left to carry out the order that he had hoped to pass off on someone else. But he lost his courage. He kept the Mormon leaders as prisoners, but he did not shoot them.

It is rare for a military officer to refuse a direct command from a superior officer. But General Doniphan was certain he was right, so he acted nobly and took his chances. Perhaps he knew the kind of coward he was dealing with. When General Lucas later wrote his report to the governor, he didn't even mention the trial or the death order.

Lucas also later reported that his troops had been well behaved and under control. But the truth was, over the next few days his army turned into a mob. They beat many of the Saints, and killed several men. They destroyed houses. They trampled crops and shot cattle for sport.

General Lucas also forced the Saints to surrender, give up their weapons, and sign away their rights to their own property. His troops took Joseph Smith home long enough to collect a few of his belongings. But when little Joseph III, Joseph's son, clung to his father's leg and cried, a soldier waved his sword and told him to get away "or I will run you through."

Hyrum Smith, who was sick in bed, was dragged out and

arrested. Soldiers placed him and Joseph and the other leaders in covered wagons to take them away to jail. The
Prophet's mother and youngest sister, Lucy, having heard
that Joseph and Hyrum were to be shot, ran to the wagons.
They were able to grasp Joseph's and Hyrum's hands, each for
a moment, before soldiers forced them to leave.

All the Saints watched as the wagons rolled away. Rain
was still pouring down. In the gloom, the members feared not
only the loss of their leaders but the destruction of the
Church itself.

Two days later, General Clark arrived. The Saints tried to
talk with him, hoping that he might be more reasonable than
General Lucas. But Clark promptly arrested fifty-six addi-
tional Church leaders. Then he assembled the Saints and
addressed them. Among other things, he told them, "You
have always been the aggressors—you have brought your-
selves these difficulties."

And he left no hope for the leaders: "Do not imagine for
a moment—do not let it enter your minds that they will be
delivered, or that you will see their faces again, for their fate
is fixed—their die is cast—their doom is sealed."

Needless to say, the words cut the Saints deeply and made
them angry but also left them near despair. All the same,
they refused to lose hope that the Lord would somehow save
them.

Contrary to General Clark's prediction, all the leaders
eventually gained their freedom. Not one lost his life or was
convicted of a crime. The Church had survived one of its
darkest hours. But none of that would have been possible had
it not been for the courage of one friend—General Alexander

Doniphan—who defied an order that his conscience told him he must not carry out.

For further reading, see Donna Hill, Joseph Smith, the First Mormon *(New York: Doubleday, 1977), pp. 237–41; Parley P. Pratt,* Autobiography of Parley P. Pratt *(Salt Lake City: Deseret Book, 1975), pp. 187–88.*

16

Joseph Silences the Guards

After the surrender of the Saints at Far West, many of the Church leaders were held prisoner while a court of inquiry met to review what had happened. The court would decide whether a trial of the Mormon leaders was justified.

But the court of inquiry, with Judge Austin A. King presiding, had a strange way of doing things. Every time the defense presented the name of a witness to tell the Mormons' side of the story, the witness was chased down, arrested, and held with the other prisoners. Before long the defense lawyers, one of whom was Alexander Doniphan, recognized that justice would not be done here. The only hope was to go on to a trial and hope for a better judge.

Joseph Smith and several other men were imprisoned together in an old log courthouse in Richmond, Missouri. Winter had come on harsh and bitter. The jail was crowded, gloomy, and cold. The prisoners, all chained to each other, were forced to sleep on the floor, with little bedding. The food was disgusting, and the men were forced to eat it with their fingers. Poor Sidney Rigdon, suffering with illness and fever, was given no special help, except that his daughter, Athalia, who was married to another of the prisoners, George

Robinson, was allowed to come inside to look after her father.

In this degrading situation one night, Joseph Smith showed what kind of man he was. With Athalia Robinson present, the guards began to brag about the terrible things they had done to the Mormons in Far West. The stories got worse and worse. The guards, using filthy language, claimed they had robbed, raped, and killed many of the Saints.

Parley Pratt, one of the Twelve Apostles, suffered through all this with the others. He listened until he was disgusted and was thinking that he ought to rise up and tell the guards what he thought of them. But Joseph Smith was the one who rose to his feet. He spoke to the guards in a voice that was like "the roaring of a lion":

"SILENCE, ye fiends of the infernal pit. In the name of Jesus Christ I rebuke you, and command you to be still; I will not live another minute and hear such language. Cease such talk, or you or I die THIS INSTANT!"

The Prophet, in his chains, stood straight and tall. The guards, frightened and humbled, backed away and actually begged Joseph's forgiveness. They remained quiet during the rest of the night.

Later, remembering the experience, Parley Pratt wrote that he had seen judges in the courts of England, and he had watched as congressmen had created laws in Washington. He had also imagined kings and royal courts, but, he said: "dignity and majesty have I seen but *once*, as it stood in chains, at midnight, in a dungeon in an obscure village of Missouri."

When the court of inquiry ended, Parley and several others continued to be held in the Richmond jail on charges of treason and murder. Joseph and Hyrum Smith were taken with some other men to a jail in Liberty, Missouri. A long winter of misery would follow, but no one who had been in the Richmond jail on that dramatic night—including the guards—would ever forget that they had seen, once in their lives, the power of a prophet.

For further reading, see Parley P. Pratt, Autobiography of Parley P. Pratt *(Salt Lake City: Deseret Book, 1975), pp. 210–11.*

17

The Flight from Far West

Joseph Smith, along with five fellow Church leaders, spent a long, difficult winter in the Liberty jail. Conditions were degrading, almost inhuman, but for Joseph the worst part was knowing that his friends and family were suffering and he could do nothing to help them. When Joseph reached the point of despair one spring day, he finally cried out, "O God, where art thou?"

The answer came in a revelation from the Lord: "Know thou, my son, that all these things shall give thee experience, and shall be for thy good. The Son of Man hath descended below them all. Art thou greater than he?"

These words comforted Joseph, and they have comforted many others throughout the history of the Church. But Joseph received no promise that the misery was over. Little did the Saints know, in fact, what great challenges lay ahead.

Church members had agreed to leave the state of Missouri in the spring, but that had not been good enough for many of the old settlers. They continued to torment and harass the Mormons who didn't move on. Before decent weather could come, even though food and warm clothing were in short supply, most of the Saints felt they had to begin their trek eastward, toward Illinois. The weather was still cold, many were sick, and everyone suffered, but children were hit the hardest. Many were buried along the way.

One of the exiles from Far West was Martha Thomas. In the late winter of 1839, Martha was thirty-one. She and her husband, Daniel, had five children. She had watched the previous fall as wagons had rolled away, carrying Joseph Smith and other Church leaders to jail. And then she had watched as armed men had arrested her husband. But Daniel had been set free just in time to arrive home and load the family's belongings onto their wagon. Snow was still on the ground, but the Thomases knew they had no choice but to get away from Far West.

So, on February 14, Martha and Daniel set out for Quincy, Illinois. The Thomases' five children walked across the frozen prairie for more than a hundred miles. The wagon was too full and the load too heavy for them to ride. Martha described the children's pain: "The snow was about six inches deep. The children all barefoot but the eldest boy. To hear them cry at night with their feet cracked open and the blood oozing out was a grievous thing for a mother to bear. I often would grease [their feet at night]."

It was a terrible journey, but Brigham Young, the president of the Quorum of the Twelve Apostles, led the way in looking out for the needs of the Saints. He and the other apostles set up stations all along the way, with food and assistance available. If it hadn't been for this careful planning, many of the travelers would have starved.

When the Thomases finally reached the Mississippi River, they learned they would have to wait to cross. Many of the Saints had arrived at the river, more than the ferry could keep up with. As the Thomases settled down for their wait, a man Martha called "Brother Bronson" called all the men in the area together. He explained to them that there were still many families in Far West whose lives were in danger. The old settlers were warning that if the remaining Saints didn't leave soon, they would all be shot. But the remaining Saints were poor and didn't have any wagons. They had no way to leave. Brother Bronson asked the men if any of them would offer their wagons to be taken back to Far West.

Daniel came back from the meeting and asked Martha what she thought. It took her no time at all to decide. "Well, dump the things out by that log," she said.

The family unpacked the wagon, and Martha watched her husband drive it off to send to those in greater need. She and her family could do nothing but sit down and wait for a chance to cross the river. She didn't say so in her account, but she must have been very worried. She did mention that she was not feeling well, but she didn't explain why.

Some friends built a little shelter for Martha out of poles and quilts, with one side left open so the heat of an open fire could reach her. "I have often thought the Queen never enjoyed such a bedroom," she later joked. But she spent only one night in that little shelter. The next morning she learned that her family could cross the Mississippi. Her children helped her carry the family's belongings onto the ferry, and they floated across the mile-wide river. Big chunks of ice were still flowing with the current, making the crossing a frightening experience, but Martha praised the Lord when the ferry arrived safely.

Getting across the river didn't solve all of the Thomases' problems, however. Daniel and his oldest son, Morgan, had stayed on the Missouri side because they had not been able to get their cow across a boggy creek bottom and up to the ferry in time for the passage. They hoped to cross later that evening.

As night fell, Martha didn't know where to go. Those who had wagons drove on ahead toward Quincy, but she had no way to travel. She also wanted to wait for Daniel to catch up so her family could stay together. So she and her children waited by the river in the cold and dark. They wrapped themselves in quilts and hoped that the boat would arrive safely and that Daniel and Morgan would be on it. For the first time, Martha couldn't hold back her tears.

Then a man rode by and told her that he had located a "house" and the Thomases were welcome to use half of it. The house, he said, was twelve feet square. Each couple had five children, so there would be fourteen people. He laughed and told her they would have plenty of standing room. He waited until he could hear the ferry approaching, and then, promising to send a wagon and team back for her, he rode on.

Martha waited for the ferry to land. What a relief it was to see Daniel and Morgan get off! Martha and Daniel rejoiced in finding each other. Then they took their children to a near-by camp, where they set up another little shelter and again waited.

The man who had come by earlier soon kept his promise. About ten o'clock another man drove a wagon into camp. The driver said he was there to carry the Thomases to the little log house.

When they reached the house that night, they found, of course, that it was very crowded. But it was also warm and safe. The Thomases were greatly relieved, and they thanked the Lord to be inside.

Just a few days later, Martha Thomas gave birth to a son.

All through this ordeal, Martha Thomas had known that she would soon be having her baby. She had known it as she and her family crossed the state of Missouri, known it when she gave up her wagon, known it as she waited by the river to cross, known it as she watched for her husband, alone on the other side. Many years later, when she finally wrote her story, she remembered the suffering of her children, the goodness of those who had built her bedroom out of poles and blankets, and the worry about her husband and son crossing the river safely. What she never mentioned was her own suffering.

For further reading, see Kenneth W. Godfrey, Audrey M. Godfrey, and Jill Mulvay Derr, Women's Voices *(Salt Lake City: Deseret Book, 1982), pp. 84–96.*

18

Brigham Young's Mission to England

As the Saints fled from Missouri in the spring of 1839, Brigham Young was faced with a hard decision. The Lord had revealed to Joseph Smith the summer before that the apostles were to serve a mission to England. They were to depart, leaving from the Far West temple site, on April 26, 1839. That hardly seemed a good time for most of the leaders of the Church to abandon the suffering Saints. And yet, Brigham was not one to ignore a direct call from the Lord.

Brigham, who was in Illinois by then, knew that a trip back into Missouri would be dangerous, but he felt he must obey the Lord. So he asked the other apostles to join him, and they rode the two hundred miles back to Far West, held a brief ceremony, and "took their leave" for their missions.

The apostles hoped the way would be opened for them now that they could soon depart for England. But first they had to get their families settled somewhere. As it turned out, their hardships had just begun.

All the brethren returned to Illinois and began the hard work of establishing the city that would be called Nauvoo. Brigham Young found a shabby log house on the Iowa side of the Mississippi River and moved his family in. The other

apostles found similar housing or began to build log cabins. The apostles were eager to get going, but when the summer heat came on, almost all the Saints began to fall ill. The mosquitoes in the wetlands around Nauvoo carried malaria, a disease that made people deathly sick.

On July 2, Joseph Smith met with the apostles. He blessed both the men and their wives, and he set them apart for their missions. Every one of the apostles was sick with malaria, and so were their families, but the men prepared to go.

Wilford Woodruff, sick as he was, got out of bed on the morning of August 8. He blessed his wife, Phoebe, who was very sick, and then he embraced her. He knew he was leaving her with little food, a rundown cabin to live in, and a sick family. Phoebe, according to Brother Woodruff, accepted his departure with the courage that "becomes a saint."

Brigham Young waited until his wife, Mary Ann, delivered a baby daughter. Mary Ann was still very sick with malaria, but ten days after the birth, Brigham left home. Since he could hardly walk because of his own illness, he asked a brother to take him on horseback to the ferry. He vowed to go to England or "die trying." But Brigham had a promise from the Prophet: "If you will go, your family shall live, and you shall live." Brigham trusted in that promise.

When Brigham and Heber Kimball left Nauvoo together, each had only one wornout suit to wear. Brigham had wrapped himself in a quilt, because he had no coat. Heber Kimball's wife, Vilate, and his children were all sick, except for one young son who was barely big enough to carry water to the house. But Heber hugged everyone and said good-bye.

Brigham Young and Heber Kimball got into a wagon and started to ride away. Heber felt so awful to be leaving his family behind, in their sickness and poverty, that he felt as though "his inmost parts would melt." Asking the wagon driver to stop, he said to Brigham, "This is pretty tough, isn't it; let's rise up and give them a cheer."

The two got up in the wagon, waved their hats over their heads, and shouted, "Hurrah, hurrah for Israel." Mary Ann Young was with Vilate Kimball, and the two came to the cabin door. They shouted, "Good-bye, God bless you."

The apostles told the driver to go on then, and Heber felt much better. "I felt a spirit of joy and gratitude," he later wrote, "having had the satisfaction of seeing my wife standing upon her feet, instead of leaving her in bed, knowing well that I should not see [my family] again for two or three years."

Brigham and Heber made slow progress at first. Their journey to Kirtland, Ohio, took seven weeks. Along the way, they stopped to preach, but they also had to rest and recover from their continued illness.

The two apostles had started out with only thirteen dollars and fifty cents between them, but they decided to ride the stagecoach for as long as their money held out. Each time they bought tickets, however, they found they had enough money to pay for the next part of their trip. Brigham accused Heber of putting money in the trunk, but Heber said he had done no such thing. When the travelers arrived in Kirtland, they still had fifty cents left, but they figured out that they had spent eighty-seven dollars—from a purse that had contained only thirteen dollars and fifty cents.

Brigham said that he didn't know how this had occurred, "except by some unseen agent from the Heavenly world." And so he knew that the Lord was with them.

But the trials didn't end.

The apostles remained in Kirtland for two weeks and then took a steamer on Lake Erie to New York. In New York City, several of the apostles gathered, ready to sail to England. One day, while waiting to raise money for the voyage, Brigham leaped from a ferry boat onto a dock. He was still weak from his illness, and he slipped and hit his shoulder, dislocating it. He asked two of the brethren to hold him down while Parley Pratt pulled on his arm. Brigham guided the bone into place with his other hand. His friends then helped him to his feet, but after walking a few steps, he fainted from the pain. The shoulder continued to give him trouble for many months afterward.

The apostles were worried about their families, but their wives wrote careful letters, revealing little about their conditions. In reality, the first winter was terrible for Mary Ann Young. At one point, out of food, she wrapped her baby in a blanket and boarded a ferry. She arrived in Nauvoo cold and exhausted and still very sick. There she found a bishop, received a few potatoes and a little flour, and gratefully returned across the river to feed her children. Fortunately, conditions gradually improved for her from that time on.

The apostles finally sailed from New York in the spring of 1840. Brigham must have felt that the worst was finally over. His shoulder was improving, and he was recovering from his illness. But the voyage was very rough, and now he was struck with seasickness. It took a whole month to cross the ocean, and during that time Brigham could rarely lift his head from the bunk. The other apostles suffered just as much.

By the time the brethren landed in England, they were

weak and exhausted from all they had been through. The malaria, the separation from their families, and the hard travel had robbed them of their strength. And now, a month of constant seasickness during the voyage had left them looking almost like skeletons. But they were filled with determination. Brigham felt the power of the Spirit that Joseph had promised him. "I gave a loud shout of hosannah," he recorded. "I felt the chains were broken, and the bands that were upon me were burst asunder."

The apostles began their work with devotion. What followed was one of the greatest missionary experiences in the history of the Church. The apostles had met their test, and now the blessings poured down upon them. Thousands of British converts came into the Church, and most of them eventually crossed the ocean and settled in Nauvoo. Many became great Church leaders.

The apostles, who had arrived sick and worn down, proved themselves to be men of power. Brigham's great commitment to the cause of truth only deepened. When he returned to his family in the summer of 1841, as promised by Joseph Smith, his wife and children were alive and well. Joseph now pronounced a revelation in which the Lord told Brigham: "It is no more required at your hands to leave your family as in times past, for your offering is acceptable to me."

Brigham recorded in his journal, with his poor spelling, "This evening I am with my love alone by my fireside for the first time for years. We injoi it and feel to prase the Lord." Certainly Brigham had earned a little rest and joy. What he didn't know was that three years later Joseph Smith would be murdered. Then Brigham, tested and proven, would be ready for an even greater challenge: the leadership of the entire Church.

For further reading, see Leonard J. Arrington, Brigham Young: American Moses *(New York: Knopf, 1985), pp. 70–97; Eugene England,* Brother Brigham *(Salt Lake City: Bookcraft, 1980), pp. 34–61; James B. Allen, Ronald K. Esplin, David J. Whittaker,* Men with a Mission *(Salt Lake City: Deseret Book, 1992), pp. 54–83.*

19

Joseph and Hyrum Come Home

Joseph Smith was in Iowa. Nauvoo was still home for most of the Saints, but huge troubles had come—the same old troubles that had followed the Mormons everywhere. In just five years Nauvoo had grown to be the biggest city in Illinois, larger than Chicago. More Church members were gathering there all the time. That meant political power for the Saints, and the old settlers of Illinois didn't like that.

And then, in the spring of 1844, Joseph Smith made a crucial decision. A local newspaper had been printing what he considered vicious lies against him and the Church. As the mayor of Nauvoo, he declared the paper a "nuisance," so the city council shut the operation down and wrecked the printing press.

Now the Church's enemies felt they had a just cause for driving the Mormons out. Local militias began to prepare for war, and the Saints in Nauvoo began to dig trenches and prepare for attack. The governor of Illinois, Thomas Ford, wrote to Joseph, demanding that he and his brother Hyrum, along with other leaders, report to Carthage, Illinois, for trial. He promised that if they would turn themselves in, he would guarantee their safety.

Joseph wrote Governor Ford that he would be happy to stand trial, if a fair trial were possible. But that wasn't likely. He was certain that if he and Hyrum gave themselves up, they would be murdered.

Joseph and Hyrum, with the help of their friend and cousin Porter Rockwell, made a dangerous night crossing of the flooding Mississippi River in a leaky little boat. They stayed at a home in Montrose, the Mormon settlement on the Iowa side of the river, as they planned their escape to the Great Basin in the West—the place where the Saints would eventually migrate and establish Salt Lake City. Porter Rockwell crossed the river again, carrying messages to Emma and orders to bring back good horses for the escape.

Joseph believed that the people of Illinois, who had grown to hate their Mormon neighbors as much as the Missourians had, wanted only him and his brother. He thought that if he and Hyrum left Illinois, the old settlers and the governor would be satisfied.

But back in Nauvoo, the Saints were terrified. They knew that mobs were threatening, and they knew that Joseph and Hyrum had left. Some didn't understand that the brothers were trying to save their friends. They thought that Joseph and Hyrum were only trying to save themselves, and called them cowards.

Even Emma wanted Joseph to turn himself in. She believed Governor Ford's promise and thought that this trial would be like the others before. Joseph had always done well when he was allowed to plead his case. At the worst, she thought, Joseph might be in jail for a time, but she believed no court could find him guilty of any serious crime. Emma sent a message with Porter Rockwell, asking her husband to come home.

When Joseph received the message, along with an account of what some of the Saints were saying, he was hurt. He told Hyrum and Porter Rockwell, "If my life is of no value to my friends, it is of none to me." He asked Porter for advice.

Porter said that Joseph knew best, and whatever the decision, he would always support him. So Joseph turned to Hyrum and asked him, as the older brother, what they should do. "Let us go back and give ourselves up, and see the thing out," Hyrum told him.

Joseph thought for a moment and then said sadly, "If you go back, I will go with you, but we shall be butchered."

"The Lord is in it," Hyrum said. "If we live or have to die, we will be reconciled to our fate."

Joseph agreed, but he felt he knew what that fate would be. He expected to die. He crossed the river back to Nauvoo and sent a letter to Governor Ford, telling him he was on his way to Carthage.

The next morning, June 24, 1844, Joseph and Hyrum, along with Porter Rockwell, John Taylor, and other Church leaders, prepared to leave Nauvoo. The weather was mild, and the sky was blue. As they rode out of town, Joseph stopped several times and looked back. He gazed on the temple, on the lovely city he had helped to build, and on his own farm. He told his friends: "I am going like a lamb to the slaughter, but I am calm as a summer's morning. I have a conscience void of offense toward God and toward all men. If they take my life, I shall die an innocent man, and my blood shall cry from the ground for vengeance, and it shall be said of me 'He was murdered in cold blood!'"

Joseph, of course, was right. On June 27 a mob rushed the Carthage jail, where the Prophet and Hyrum were being held. The guards, actually cooperating with the attackers, allowed them to charge up the stairs and fire their rifles into the jail room. Joseph ran to the window, but a shower of bullets hit him as men fired from outside the jail. Joseph fell out the window and landed in the dust below. Hyrum lay on the floor of the jail.

Willard Richards and John Taylor had been visiting with the Smith brothers in their jail room. Willard Richards received only a slight wound, but several bullets struck John Taylor, and for a time it seemed likely he would die. He survived, however, and went on to lead the Church as its third President.

But Joseph and Hyrum were dead.

Their bodies, each in a rough pine box, were carried back in a wagon to Nauvoo. An honor guard and a brass band met the wagon and led a procession through the streets, where all the people of the city lined up to watch. The next day, ten thousand Saints waited in line to walk past the caskets and pay their last respects. Grief hung in the air, and to many it seemed that the Church would never survive.

But Hyrum had been right when he had told his younger brother that if they died the Lord was "in it." The Lord had delivered Joseph and Hyrum years before from the Liberty jail, and he might have done the same at Carthage. But now their work was complete.

The two martyrs sealed their testimonies with their own blood. From that time on they stood as symbols to a people who had many more trials ahead of them.

For further reading, see B. H. Roberts, A Comprehensive

History of the Church, *6 vols. (Provo, Utah: Brigham Young University Press, 1965),* 2:246–51; *Joseph Smith,* History of The Church of Jesus Christ of Latter-day Saints, *7 vols. (Salt Lake City: Deseret Book, 1951),* 6:549–57; *Donna Hill,* Joseph Smith, the First Mormon *(New York: Doubleday, 1977), pp. 398–404.*

20

The Mantle of the Prophet

It took nearly three weeks for news of Joseph and Hyrum's deaths to reach Brigham Young in Boston. Most of the twelve apostles were on missions in the eastern part of the United States. When they learned of the murders, they hurried back to Nauvoo.

What they found in Nauvoo was confusion. Once the funeral for Joseph and Hyrum had ended, the questions had come: Who was in charge? Could the Church even stay together?

Some thought that the prophet's oldest son, Joseph Smith III, should be the next prophet and President of the Church. A number of leaders spoke on their own behalf. Sidney Rigdon had disconnected himself from the Church the year before and was living in Pittsburgh. But now he returned and said that he had seen a vision that he should lead. He was, after all, the only remaining member of the First Presidency.

When Brigham first received the news of Joseph's death, he wondered whether the keys of the kingdom had been lost from the earth. But he remembered a letter Joseph had written him from the Liberty Jail. Joseph had instructed the Twelve to elect a president—the senior member of the quorum. If anything happened to Joseph, he explained, the men who held the keys of the apostleship would lead the Church.

As Brigham thought of this, he slapped his knee and said, "The keys of the kingdom are right here with the Church." So he hurried back to Nauvoo to see to it that the Church didn't fall apart. He had loved Joseph, and was completely loyal to him. His grief was overwhelming. But now he knew what course the Lord wanted the Church to follow. He put aside his sorrow and went to work.

As soon as Brigham got to Nauvoo, he met with the other apostles who had arrived. A general meeting of all the Church members was called for the next morning. Sidney Rigdon would be allowed to present his case for leadership first.

The next morning, Sidney Rigdon spoke for an hour and a half. He argued that he should lead the Church until the day that Joseph III was grown and ready to take over the leadership himself. But everyone there knew that Rigdon had broken with Joseph Smith the year before, and most were suspicious of him.

When Brigham Young finally took his turn to speak, his voice was penetrating and powerful. He taught the Saints what Joseph had taught him, and what he had told the other apostles the night before, "I don't care who leads the church . . . ; but one thing I must know, and that is what God says about it. I have the keys and the means of obtaining the mind of God on the subject. . . . How often has Joseph said to the Twelve, 'I have laid the foundation and you must build thereon, for upon your shoulders the kingdom rests.'"

Brigham's arguments were persuasive. But more powerful

than his words was the spirit with which he spoke. Many people who were there that day said that when Brigham spoke, they heard Joseph's voice. Looking at Brigham, they saw the martyred prophet's face, even his physical presence. They took it as a sign that God had placed the mantle of leadership on Brigham's shoulders, showing them who should lead the Church.

One man, George Romney, late in his life, bore testimony of what he saw that day: "When Brigham got up the mantle of Joseph Smith fell upon him. It was Joseph's voice; it was Joseph's appearance, and I testify to you, if I never again do so on this earth, in the presence of God and angels, that this is verily the truth."

Joseph had fallen, but the Church had not. Brigham Young was the powerful leader needed to take the Saints through the terrible trials to come. That day, August 8, 1844, the members of the Church sustained Brigham Young and the Twelve as those holding the keys to the kingdom. God had shown them the course they must take.

For further reading, see Eugene England, Brother Brigham *(Salt Lake City: Bookcraft, 1980), pp. 69–75; Leonard J. Arrington,* Brigham Young: American Moses *(New York: Knopf, 1985), pp. 113–16.*

21

Miracles in the Poor Camp

After the death of Joseph Smith, the Saints tried to make peace with the people of Illinois. For about a year an uneasy stand-off persisted, but late in the summer of 1845, mob violence broke out. Once again, the Saints tried to make it through another winter, and once again the mobs were not satisfied to let them stay just until spring.

The Saints pushed ahead to finish the inside of their temple so that ordinances could be performed. Even as the members hurried to receive their endowments, they were preparing to leave their beloved city. Early in February the great exodus began.

The first groups to cross the Mississippi River did so on ferries, but bitter cold set in and ice formed across the river. The ice helped thousands to cross. The cold, however, was a mixed blessing. The suffering was terrible in the camps across the river. Still, most of the Saints survived and then pushed on as the weather improved.

As the wagon trains reached the top of the hill across the river, the Saints would take one last look at their lost city and at the gleaming white temple. Many reported in their journals the heartache in saying good-bye to everything they had worked so hard to build.

Illness struck many of the members, especially the children, and the ordinary events of life became great trials. Babies were born in temporary shelters, in tents, or in wagons. Eliza R. Snow said that sisters would walk all day, through any weather, and then prepare meals at night without so much as a tent for cover. Then they would make their beds under wagons that contained everything they owned.

All during the summer of 1846, thousands of Mormons worked their way slowly across Iowa. But a few hundred of the Saints remained in Nauvoo. They were too poor to buy provisions and wagons, or too sick to travel. For a time the old settlers left them alone, but toward the end of the summer the pressure increased again. More than six hundred Church members crossed the Mississippi River to avoid further troubles, but that was as far as they could go.

Many of the men in this "poor camp" went to nearby towns and farms to look for work. Others simply tried to rest and recover from their illnesses. All of them watched their supplies gradually disappear. The adults survived on almost nothing as they tried to keep their children alive. Soon, they knew, they would all starve.

And then, a miracle occurred—or maybe it would be better to say, two miracles occurred.

One day, quail began to drop out of the sky into the poor camp. Even small children could easily grab them. Some of the birds, apparently exhausted from a long flight, flopped directly into shelters and tents.

The quail were everywhere, thick on the ground. The people caught *thousands* of them. And these people were too weak and sick to chase the birds. They wouldn't have caught anything if the quail hadn't been so easy to gather up.

For these poor Saints, who didn't know where they would find food when their provisions ran out, the quail were an answer to prayers. What they didn't know was that another kind of miracle was occurring at Winter Quarters—the place where the migrating Saints were gathering just beyond the western border of Iowa.

Brigham Young heard about the Saints trapped in the poor camp. He called for volunteers to go back across Iowa with wagons and supplies to gather up the Church members who were stranded on the banks of the Mississippi River.

Men who had just labored all summer to get their own families to Winter Quarters must have thought twice about turning back. It was a round trip of more than five hundred miles, with winter not far off. But volunteers stepped forward and agreed to go. After all, the people in the poor camp were their brothers and sisters.

A wagon train hurried back to the poor camp, gathered up the stranded people there, and then traveled back across Iowa. Most of the people of the poor camp were saved.

Perhaps most amazing, such miracles of bravery would prove to be common, not exceptional, as the Mormons continued their trek from Winter Quarters to the West in the following years.

For further reading, see B. H. Roberts, A Comprehensive History of the Church, *6 vols. (Provo, Utah: Brigham Young University Press, 1965), 3:134–36.*

22

Hosea Stout's Great Loss

The first wagon trains that pushed westward across Iowa met with great hardship. Cold and snow made travel very slow, and springtime didn't make things much easier. Heavy rains combined with melting snow to turn the dirt roads to deep mud. Rivers flooded, and the Saints had to repair or rebuild almost every bridge they came to.

The trip was so difficult that many of the Saints didn't reach Winter Quarters until late in the summer. There they settled in, hoping to survive the winter so they could move on to the Great Basin the following year.

Among the Saints who reached Winter Quarters that summer was a man named Hosea Stout. He had been chief of police and an important leader in Nauvoo. But now he had spent many months on the open prairies with nothing but a tent to shelter him and his wife, Miranda, and their two sons. Every day had been a trial.

Hosea had responsibilities and worries. He was in charge of hauling the guns of the Nauvoo Legion, the militia that he had been part of, but he didn't have enough wagons. The company he traveled with was short of food and other supplies. Even one of his best friends, a brother in the gospel, seemed to turn against him for reasons he couldn't understand.

But Hosea's greatest worry was the sickness of his family. In Missouri, during the awful winter following the extermination order, Hosea had lost his young wife to illness. A baby daughter, his only child at the time, had also died. He had married again, in Nauvoo, but now once again he was running from a mob while his family was sick.

Hosea watched his baby son weaken daily, and on May 8, 1846, little Hyrum finally died in his father's arms. Hosea was crushed, and also terribly worried: he couldn't provide proper food for his pregnant wife and older son, and he couldn't get them in out of the weather. They, too, were now frail and in great danger.

All the same, the Stouts pushed on with their wagon train. By the middle of June, Hosea began to believe that his three-year-old son, Hosea, Jr., would recover. But a heavy storm on Thursday, June 25, soaked everything the family owned, including the little boy's bed. The child's condition worsened and soon became hopeless.

Little Hosea passed through a time of agony, but on Sunday he finally slept peacefully. On Monday he died. The members of the wagon train waited long enough to bury the child, but then they traveled on for four more miles before stopping for the day. That night Hosea Stout wrote in his journal:

> Thus died my only son and one too on whom
> I had placed my own name and was truly the
> dearest object of my heart. Gone too in the

midst of affliction sorrow & disappointment in the wild solitary wilderness. . . .

I have once lost a companion for life and [was] left without a bosom friend. . . . But not then did I feel the loss or mourn as for an only son. This last loss. This loss of my only son. This my hopes for comfort in my old age. This darling object of my heart gone seemed to cap the climax of all my former misfortunes and seemed more than else to leave me utterly hopeless.

Before Hosea stopped writing, he expressed his appreciation for the kindness everyone had offered him and his wife. Then, the next day, he wrote only: "To day all the men who possibly could leave their camps went down to work at the bridge I did not go but staid at home to fix up and to arrainge my affairs as they were much out of order."

The day after that Brother Stout began his journal entry by saying, simply, "To day I worked on the bridge."

He had given himself one day to grieve, one day to set his life in order. Then, in spite of all the pain, he and Miranda pushed ahead with the others. One can only guess what Miranda was also feeling that day, still very sick, pregnant, and now without either of her sons.

Hosea's journal seldom mentions after that the grief he must have continued to suffer. But he still had reason to hope. Miranda was holding on, along with the baby she was expecting. A new life—another child—could give them a new start.

But then, on September 26, Miranda gave birth to a stillborn child. Shortly afterward, she died herself. Hosea had lost another entire family.

Hosea Stout did not write much in his journal for some time. He was sick himself for a while. But finally, on November 24, he completed a log cabin to the point that he could move inside. That night he wrote again of all he had suffered and lost. He was angry with the mobs who twice had driven him from his home. And he was angry with a government that had done nothing to stop the mobs. Even deeper than his anger was his heartbreak and loneliness. Yet he finished his journal entry by saying that through all these "adverse changes" and trials, he had never once regretted following the "voice of the spirit."

And he didn't give up.

Hosea Stout survived the winter and the migration across the plains. He became one of the great leaders in the settlement of the West. He helped establish the cotton mission in southern Utah, and he served a mission to China. With other wives, he was finally blessed with many children. And he trusted all his life that he would, after death, be reunited with the beloved wives and children he had buried along the trails, out in the "wild solitary wilderness."

For further reading, see Juanita Brooks, ed., On the Mormon Frontier: The Diary of Hosea Stout, *2 vols. (Salt Lake City: University of Utah Press, 1964), 1:121–97.*

23

The Lost Oxen

Joseph F. Smith, the son of Hyrum Smith, became the sixth President of the Church. When he was a boy, his widowed mother, Mary Fielding Smith, once taught him a lesson about prayer that he would never forget.

In the fall of 1847, Joseph F. was almost nine years old and was living in Winter Quarters. He traveled with his mother and uncle, Joseph Fielding, fifty miles to the city of St. Joseph, Missouri, to buy supplies for the winter and for their planned trip to the Great Salt Lake Valley the next spring. Little Joseph F. drove one wagon and his uncle another, each wagon pulled by four oxen. Rain fell throughout the journey, and the roads were muddy and hard to travel on.

On the way back, one morning the travelers awoke to find two of their eight oxen gone. The camp was near a little creek on an open prairie, so the oxen should have been easy to spot. Some men were camped on the other side of the creek, tending a herd of cattle. The night before, Uncle Joseph Fielding had left the oxen in their yokes so they wouldn't wander across the stream and get mixed in with the other cattle. There seemed to be no way that the oxen could have gone very far. But they had vanished.

Joseph F. and his uncle spent the whole morning looking for the lost animals. The two of them tramped through the deep grass, wet with dew, and wore themselves out with the work. But they saw no sign of the oxen.

When Joseph F. returned to camp he found his mother on her knees, praying. He heard her pleading with Lord not to leave them in this helpless condition. One team would never be able to pull the heavy wagon through the mud, and the food and supplies were so important for the trip across the plains.

Joseph Fielding returned a few minutes later and told his sister, "Well, Mary, the cattle are gone!"

But Sister Smith seemed unconcerned, almost cheerful. She told the two Josephs, "I will just take a walk out and see if I can find the cattle." Joseph Fielding threw up his hands in astonishment. And Joseph F. couldn't have been more surprised, as he expressed it, had the Missouri River "suddenly turned to run up stream."

But Sister Smith walked toward the creek, just a short distance from the camp. It was the one place where Joseph F. and his uncle were sure they could see everything already. When Mary got to the creek, a cattle driver called across and said he had seen the oxen moving in the opposite direction at sunrise that morning. But Mary ignored the man and continued on her way.

Soon she was waving for Joseph F. and her brother to join her. The two got up from their greatly delayed breakfast and ran to her. Joseph F. described what he saw:

> There I saw our oxen fastened to a clump of willows growing in the bottom of a deep gulch

which had been washed out of the sandy bank
of the river by the little spring creek, perfectly
concealed from view. We were not long in
releasing them from bondage and getting back
to our camp, where the other cattle had been
fastened to the wagon wheels all the morning,
and we were soon on our way home rejoicing.

Mary had known where to look for the oxen because the
Lord had shown her.

Joseph F., remembering this experience many years later,
said, "It made an indelible impression upon my mind, and
has been a source of comfort, assurance and guidance to me
throughout all of my life."

For further reading, see Joseph Fielding Smith, Life of Joseph F.
Smith *(Salt Lake City: Deseret Book, 1938), pp. 131–34.*

24

A Harvest of Faith

Brigham Young led the first company of Saints to the Great Salt Lake Valley. The wagons arrived late in July of 1847. This was an advance company, sent to prepare the way for those who would follow. When these first Saints arrived, they wasted no time in getting to work. They knew they had to prepare the way for thousands of their brothers and sisters who would be arriving the next summer. Above all, they had to have food ready and waiting.

These pioneers soon learned that farming in the desert valleys of the Great Basin was not going to be easy. The land was dry and hard. In time, Mormon settlers would build irrigation canals to bring water from the nearby mountain streams. But for the present, they planted a few crops in the hopes of having a small harvest even so late in the season. Then they fenced off a large field and began the backbreaking work of preparing the ground for planting the following spring. They broke their plows and wore down their cattle, but they stuck with the job. A mild winter allowed them to work the soil through most of the year. They planted thousands of acres of wheat.

By spring, these advance settlers were almost out of food.

They had little beef, since all their cattle were needed for milk or for work, and the supplies they had carried with them were almost gone. The whole community was put on rations, and people survived any way they could. They learned from the Indians, for instance, that the roots of thistles and sego lilies, while not exactly tasty, could be eaten. Each family planted a garden, but as the people waited and hoped for an early harvest, they also knew that if their crops failed, they would starve.

The Saints watched as the wheat sprouted in the big field. Finally the end to their hunger seemed to be in sight. Then disaster struck.

As the first settlers had entered the valley the summer before, they had noticed huge black crickets along the river. They hadn't thought much about them then, but now, nine months later, they could think of nothing else. Millions of the creatures came hopping down out of the mountains and began feasting on the young wheat plants. Nothing, it seemed, could stop them.

The settlers tried to bury the crickets, fight them with their hands, wash them away, even burn them, but nothing worked. Every day more and more of the beautiful green fields turned black, then brown, as the crickets ate the plants down to the ground and then marched on. There was nothing the farmers could do. They kept fighting the crickets, but they knew their efforts were hopeless. How would they stay alive? They needed to find some answer and find it soon.

Many of these people had broken ground and built homes in Missouri, only to be driven away by mobs. Then they had done the same in Nauvoo, once again to be forced out. Now they had trudged a thousand miles away from civilization to a place they thought no one wanted—a place where they could live in peace. And now they were being threatened once again with destruction—this time by an insect.

The people—men, women, and children all together—continued to fight for their crops even when they knew they couldn't win. And they prayed. Every one of them must have wondered when the Lord would ever decide that they had suffered enough.

Then a cloud appeared in the sky—or at least that was what it seemed to be. But it moved too fast to be a cloud. It turned out to be thousands of seagulls, flying in from the Great Salt Lake. As the gulls landed in the fields, the settlers first thought the birds were also after the wheat sprouts. Instead, they began to eat the crickets.

To those early Saints the birds seemed like white-winged angels, but they ate like gluttons. They flew to streams and vomited up the hard body parts of the crickets. Then they came back to eat again. They kept this up for days, until the crickets were virtually gone.

The Saints watched. And they prayed again, this time to thank the Lord.

It is natural for a seagull to eat insects. It is even natural for birds to vomit the parts of the insect that are not easily digested. That part was not really a miracle. The real miracle was that the seagulls had come just in time. And the Saints knew, without a doubt, who had sent them.

For further reading, see Parley P. Pratt, Autobiography of Parley P. Pratt *(Salt Lake City: Deseret Book, 1975), pp. 363–64; B. H. Roberts,* A Comprehensive History of the Church, *6 vols. (Provo, Utah: Brigham Young University Press, 1965), 2:329–35.*

25

Sailing to Madras

While the wagon trains were rolling westward to the Great Salt Lake Valley, the Saints continued to send missionaries out to all the world. The greatest harvest of converts came from England and Wales, but missionaries were also traveling to the islands of the Pacific, to South America, and even to India. Missionaries often traveled on riverboats and ships, and some very exciting missionary experiences occurred on those voyages.

In 1853, one group of nine missionaries sailed to Calcutta, India. Two of the elders, Richard Ballantyne and Robert Skelton, were then sent on to the city of Madras, on the east side of the tip of India.

India has a monsoon season, when fierce storms dump hundreds of inches of rain in just a few months. In those days, a sea voyage during a monsoon was out of the question. The two elders discovered that there would be only one more ship, the *John Brightman*, sailing to Madras before the rainy season began. Madras was hundreds of miles from Calcutta, and sailing was the best way to get there. Unfortunately, the captain of the ship, Captain Thomas Scott, didn't like Mormons and refused to take the elders on board.

Elder Ballantyne was impressed to make an unusual promise. He told Captain Scott that if he would transport the missionaries, the Lord would guarantee a safe trip. The captain accepted the bargain and let them board his ship.

To leave the port of Calcutta, a ship had to sail down the Hooghly River. It was a dangerous waterway with too much traffic. At the narrowest point, another ship appeared. It was heading directly for the *John Brightman*, and Captain Scott saw the collision coming. But Elder Ballantyne calmly assured the captain that there was no danger, and the captain was shocked when the ships seemed to steer themselves around each other. Whether the captain believed in miracles or not, he instantly became a friend to the missionaries.

The ship reached the open sea only to be battered by a hurricane all along its course to Madras. Two sailors were thrown overboard—but both were rescued. Sails tore and masts broke. Water washed over the decks. Lightning flashed all around the ship. The voyage was a terrible ordeal, but the ship stayed together and finally arrived in Madras.

When the ship put in to port safely, Captain Scott was finally convinced that Richard Ballantyne's promise had been kept. He gave Elder Ballantyne a pair of shoes. He also gave him enough money to rent a room and to print two thousand missionary pamphlets. The man who had hated Mormons was now helping missionary work for the Church get started in India.

For further reading, see Conway B. Sonne, Saints on the Seas: A Maritime History of the Mormon Migration, 1830–1890 *(Salt Lake City: University of Utah Press, 1983), pp. 7–10.*

26

"Save the People"

Brigham Young was committed to the idea that no member of the Church should suffer when other members could prevent it. No one should go hungry when others had extra. No one should ever be abandoned. That commitment was tested as the Saints moved across the prairies and mountains into the valley of the Great Salt Lake.

As thousands of Mormons struggled across America to reach their new home, missionaries in Europe, and especially in Great Britain, were baptizing thousands more. They asked these converts to leave behind homes and families and join with the Saints in Zion, and many did just that. But after crossing the Atlantic, most of the new members had little money left to make the trip from the Mississippi River to the Rocky Mountains.

To help these brothers and sisters, Brigham Young began a program called the Perpetual Emigration Fund. Members of the Church were called on to contribute money that would be used to pay for others to make the trip to the West. When those people arrived and went to work, they would pay back the costs of their travel into the fund. In this way, the fund would never run out, and no one would be left behind.

It was an excellent plan, but there was one problem. It was often difficult for people, in their poverty, to pay the fund back. That meant that the amount of money in the account slowly shrank. And with all the new converts lining up to cross the plains, it was becoming too expensive to provide wagons and teams for everyone.

Brigham's solution to this problem was a simple one. Instead of traveling by wagon, families would walk across the plains, pulling their belongings on handcarts. Many sections of the trail were easier to walk on than to drive wagons over, so the trip would take less time. And the travelers wouldn't have to worry about tending so many animals. Of course, they wouldn't be able to bring as many belongings, but most of the European immigrants hadn't brought much with them anyway.

There were problems with this plan, however. The hand-carts offered little room for food. In a storm, there was no wagon to crawl into. And small children and older people, or those who became sick, had to be pulled in the carts.

At best, traveling with the handcart companies was brutal work. But the system worked for a time.

In 1856, five handcart companies of European converts left from Iowa City, Iowa, and made their way to Salt Lake City. The first three had no serious problems. The last two weren't as fortunate. The Willie Company and the Martin Company started much later in the year. The leaders of these companies might have been wise to delay their departure until the next spring, but the Saints were anxious to move on, and they were convinced that God would protect them.

Going forward so late turned out to be a fateful decision, however. On October 1, the Willie Company left Fort

Laramie, still five hundred miles away from Salt Lake City. By that time winter storms had begun in the mountains, but the company pushed ahead anyway. The Martin Company followed on October 9.

Both companies ran into raging blizzards. The people had tried to lighten their loads so they could move faster, but in doing so they had left behind things they needed, such as heavy coats, blankets, and extra clothes. Many walked through the snow without shoes. Their clothes got wet from crossing ice-cold rivers, and then froze to their bodies. It was all they could do just to start a fire some nights.

Finally, in the middle of the worst blizzard yet, the immigrants thought they were finished. A few men went ahead, breaking their way through the snow and hoping to get help from the Saints in Salt Lake City. Meanwhile, the companies tried to survive in the mountains, but many were dying.

The men got through just as the Saints were gathering in a general conference. President Young listened to the heartbreaking news, and then he addressed the congregation:

> Many of our brethren and sisters are on the plains with handcarts. . . . They must be brought here, we must send assistance to them. . . . I want the brethren who may speak [today] to understand that their text is the people on the Plains. And the subject matter for this community is to send for them and bring them in before the winter sets in. That is my religion; that is the dictation of the Holy Ghost that I possess. It is to save the people.

President Young asked for volunteers to go back along the trail as a rescue party. The response was overwhelming. He asked for plenty of wagons, drivers, oxen, clothes, food—and he got more than he asked for. During the days and weeks to come, he continued to ask for more help, and the Saints never disappointed him or their stranded sisters and brothers.

The rescue parties fought their way through the storm that had pinned down the Willie and Martin companies. The snow was so bad that they were almost ready to turn back when two riders came out of the storm. Joseph Willie and another brother arrived at the rescuers' camp and told them that they were just a few miles away from the Willie Company, and only a day and a half away from the Martin Company. With that news, the rescuers pushed ahead once again.

Men, wagons, and supplies poured out of Salt Lake City. When they reached the stranded Saints, they were greeted as angels of mercy. More than two hundred of the handcart pioneers died, but hundreds more made it to the valley because of these rescue parties.

Patience Loader's family was in the Martin Company. When the people of this company, now aided by rescuers, reached the Sweetwater River, they saw that the ice had been broken by wagons. They had already crossed many icy rivers, and they were afraid to cross another in their weakened condition. Patience described what happened:

> Three brave men [were] there in the water packing the women and children over on their backs. Names: William Kimball, Ephraim Hanks and I think the other was James

> Ferguson. Those poor brethren was in the water nearly all day. We wanted to thank them, but they would not listen. . . . This poor Brother Kimball stayed so long in the water that he had to be taken and packed to camp, and he was a long time before he recovered, as he was chilled through, and in after life he was always afflicted with rheumatism.

The first group of the surviving immigrants arrived in the valley on a Sunday. When Brigham Young heard the news, he showed his practical side. He told the congregation: "The afternoon meeting will be omitted, for I wish the sisters to go home and prepare to give those who have just arrived a mouthful of something to eat, and to wash them and nurse them up. . . . Prayer is good, but when baked potatoes and milk are needed, prayer will not supply their place."

Later, when Brigham visited the survivors himself, he showed the deep compassion that was also part of his nature. Mary Goble Pay, then a girl of thirteen, recorded her memory of Brigham arriving at the house where she had been taken in:

> When Bro. Young came in he shook hands with us all. When he saw our condition—our feet frozen and our mother dead—tears rolled down his cheeks.
>
> The doctor amputated my toes using a saw and a butcher knife. Brigham Young promised me I would not have to have any more of my feet cut off.

And she didn't. But Brigham worried constantly until the rest of the survivors were brought in. What he saw was the commitment he had hoped for. Those who had heard his sermon and had committed to save the people never stopped working until they had brought the last ones to safety.

For further reading, see B. H. Roberts, A Comprehensive History of the Church, *6 vols. (Provo, Utah: Brigham Young University Press, 1965), 4:89–105; Wallace Stegner,* The Gathering of Zion, the Story of the Mormon Trail *(Salt Lake City: Westwater Press, 1964), pp. 221–55.*

Afterword

When we tell stories from Mormon history, we remember especially heroes and heroines—people of great faith. We tend to forget that there were also backsliders and weaklings among the early members. Most of all, there were common people who did their best and carried out their duties in a quiet way without ever being remembered in history books. In the diaries and journals from that early era, we learn that many of those quiet lives were also filled with heroism. The people survived in a very tough time, and those who held to the faith accomplished a great deal just to raise families and carry out the work of the Church.

One little story from the history of early Utah symbolizes the grit that many of the members had to discover in themselves. Robert Gardner heard a rumor that he had been called to go on a "cotton mission," and he wasn't very pleased about it. He ran a sawmill in Salt Lake City, and he had worked hard to get his business going and his family settled. Now he was being asked to give up everything to move to the deserts of southern Utah. Why? To raise cotton. Or at least to try to raise cotton. In fact, no one knew whether cotton would grow in the southern deserts at all. In truth, he didn't want to go.

Brother Gardner found George A. Smith of the Quorum of the Twelve and asked whether the rumor was true. Elder Smith said yes, that Brother Gardner's family was on the list, but the name could be removed if the Gardners didn't want to go. Still, Brigham was hoping that they would. They were needed.

Brother Gardner looked around and spat on the ground. He took off his hat, scratched his head, thought about it for a minute, and then he said, "All right."

Cotton, as it turned out, didn't do well in southern Utah. Still, Robert Gardner and his wife and children suffered through some hard seasons and tried to make a go of it. They would rather have stayed in Salt Lake City. But Brigham Young wanted their help, and Brother Gardner wasn't about to turn down the prophet.

It was that kind of commitment that kept things going until the Saints found a way to survive and prosper in a harsh environment. But it's also the same kind of commitment that keeps things going today. Modern Mormons often learn the wrong lesson from their own history. Too often, in sacrament meetings, especially around the twenty-fourth of July, speakers tell the modern Saints that they aren't as tough as those gritty pioneers, that modern members could never survive what the early Saints went through.

But that is obviously not true. The Church continues to survive in a harsh environment. Tens of thousands of young people are heading out, all across the world, to continue to carry the message that Joseph Smith brought back to the earth. Great numbers of retired couples do the same. The work of the Church—the teaching and leading and caring—goes on in every ward and branch. And heroes devote their time to "saving the people" every day, often in quiet ways.

There is still plenty of grit in the Church. We may scratch our heads, as Brother Gardner did, and wonder whether we really want to take that new calling or carry out an assignment. But we do it, and we do it in a time when the challenges have actually never been greater. Crossing the plains was tough, but living a good life in a corrupt world is also tough. Faith, nobility, goodness, love, heroism—all these qualities are still with us, and our own journals will someday give courage to those who come after us.